TRAILBLAZERS
IN SCIENCE AND TECHNOLOGY

Nikola Tesla

HARNESSING ELECTRICITY

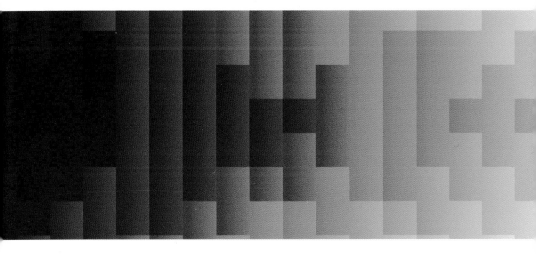

TRAILBLAZERS
IN SCIENCE AND TECHNOLOGY

Nikola Tesla

HARNESSING ELECTRICITY

Lisa Yount

CHELSEA HOUSE
An Infobase Learning Company

Chelsea House
An imprint of Infobase Learning
132 West 31st Street
New York NY 10001

Library of Congress Cataloging-in-Publication Data

Yount, Lisa.
    Nikola Tesla: harnessing electricity / Lisa Yount.
        p. cm.—(Trailblazers in science and technology)
    Includes bibliographical references and index.
    ISBN 978-1-60413-670-8
    1. Tesla, Nikola, 1856–1943—Juvenile literature. 2. Electrical engineers—United States—
Biography—Juvenile literature. 3. Inventors—United States—Biography—Juvenile literature. I. Title.
    TK140.T4Y68 2011
621.3092—dc22   2010052627

Chelsea House books are available at special discounts when purchased in bulk quantities
for businesses, associations, institutions, or sales promotions. Please call our Special Sales
Department in New York at (212) 967-8800 or (800) 322-8755.

You can find Chelsea House on the World Wide Web at http://www.infobaselearning.com

Excerpts included herewith have been reprinted by permission of the copyright holders; the
author has made every effort to contact copyright holders. The publishers will be glad to
rectify, in future editions, any errors or omissions brought to their notice.

Text design by Erika K. Arroyo
Composition by Hermitage Publishing Service
Illustrations by Bobbi McCutcheon
Photo research by Suzanne M. Tibor
Cover printed by Yurchak Printing, Landisville, Pa.
Book printed and bound by Yurchak Printing, Landisville, Pa.

Printed in the United States of America

This book is printed on acid-free paper.

for ALEC
who may also be ahead of his time
and
in memory of BRUCE HENDERSON

Contents

Preface

Trailblazers in Science and Technology is a multivolume set of biographies for young adults that profiles 10 individuals or small groups who were "trailblazers" in science—in other words, those who made discoveries that greatly broadened human knowledge and sometimes changed society or saved many lives. In addition to describing those discoveries and their effects, the books explore the qualities that made these people trailblazers, the personal relationships they formed, and way those relationships interacted with their scientific work.

What does it take to be a trailblazer, in science or any other field of human endeavor?

First, a trailblazer must have imagination: the power to envision a path where others see only expanses of jungle, desert, or swamp. Helen Taussig, Alfred Blalock, and Vivien Thomas imagined an operation that could help children whose condition everyone else thought was hopeless. Louis and Mary Leakey looked at shards of bone embedded in the rocks of an African valley and pictured in them the story of humanity's birth.

Imagination alone will not blaze a trail, however. A trailblazer must also have determination and courage, the will to keep on trudging and swinging a metaphorical machete long after others fall by the wayside. Pierre and Marie Curie stirred their witch's cauldron for day after day in a dirty shed, melting down tons of rock to extract a tiny sample of a strange new element. The women astronomers who assisted Edward Pickering patiently counted and compared white spots on thousands of photographs in order to map the universe.

Because their vision is so different from that of others, trailblazers often are not popular. They may find themselves isolated even from those who are working toward the same goals, as Rosalind Franklin did in her research on DNA. Other researchers may brand them as "outsiders" and therefore ignore their work, as mathematicians did at first with Edward Lorenz's writings on chaos theory because Lorenz's background was in meteorology (weather science), a quite different scientific discipline. Society may regard them as eccentric or worse, as happened to electricity pioneer Nikola Tesla and, to a lesser extent, genome analyst and entrepreneur Craig Venter. This separateness sometimes freed and sometimes hindered these individuals' creative paths.

On the other hand, the relationships that trailblazers do form often sustain them and enrich their work. In addition to supplying emotional and intellectual support, compatible partners of whatever type can build on one another's ideas to achieve insights that neither would have been likely to develop alone. Two married couples described in this set, the Curies and the Leakeys, not only helped each other in their scientific efforts but inspired some of their children to continue their path. Other partnerships, such as the one between Larry Page and Sergey Brin, the computer scientists-turned-entrepreneurs who founded the Internet giant Google, related strictly to business, but they were just as essential to the partners' success.

Even relationships that have an unhealthy side may prove to offer unexpected benefits. Pickering hired women such as Williamina Fleming to be his astronomical "computers" because he could pay them far less than he would have had to give men for the same work. Similarly, Alfred Blalock took advantage of Vivien Thomas's limited work choices as an African American to keep Thomas at his command in the surgical laboratory. At the same time, these instances of exploitation, so typical of the society of the times, gave the "exploited" opportunities that they would not otherwise have had. Thomas would not have contributed to lifesaving surgeries if he had remained a carpenter in Nashville, even though he might have earned more money than he did by working for Blalock. Fleming surely would never have discovered her talent for astronomy if Pickering had kept her as merely his "Scottish maid."

Competitors can form almost as close a relationship as cooperative partners, and like the irritating grain of sand in an oyster's shell that eventually yields a pearl, rivalries can inspire scientific trailblazers to heights of achievement that they might not have attained if they had worked unopposed. Tesla's competition with Thomas Edison to establish a grid of electrical power around U.S. cities stimulated as well as infuriated both men. Venter's announcement that he would produce a readout of humanity's genes sooner than the massive, government-funded Human Genome Project pushed him, as well as his rival, HGP leader Francis Collins, to greater efforts. The French virologist Luc Montagnier was spurred to refine and prove his suspicions about the virus he thought was linked to AIDS because he knew that Robert Gallo, a similar researcher in another country, was close to publishing the same conclusions.

It is our hope that the biographies in the Trailblazers in Science and Technology set will inspire young people not only to discover and nurture the trailblazer within themselves but also to trust their imagination, even when it shows them a path that others say cannot exist, yet at the same time hold it to strict standards of proof. We hope they will form supportive relationships with others who share their vision, yet will also be willing to learn from those they compete with or even dislike. Above all, we hope they will feel the curiosity about the natural world and the determination to unravel its secrets that all trailblazers share.

Acknowledgments

I would like to thank Frank K. Darmstadt for his help and suggestions, Suzie Tibor for rounding up the photographs, Bobbi McCutcheon for drawing the diagrams, my cats for keeping me company (helpfully or otherwise), and my husband, Harry Henderson, for patiently explaining the mysteries of electricity and—well—everything.

Introduction

Most people can remember a time when the electric power in their home failed, perhaps during a winter storm. For hours, or sometimes days, they found themselves at a loss. No lights . . . no radio . . . no television . . . food beginning to spoil in the dark refrigerator . . . no electric range, dishwasher, microwave oven, or toaster. Flashlights and a few other conveniences might run on batteries for a while, but batteries are soon exhausted. After that stored energy was gone, the people in the home were again forced to remember just how much of daily life depends on a steady flow of electricity.

When the power finally came on once more, the family should have given thanks to Nikola Tesla (1856–1943). Tesla, an ethnic Serb, was born in the village of Smiljan in what is now Croatia and what was then the Austrian Empire. He created the system that produces, transmits, and distributes electricity to homes and businesses throughout the world. In doing so, many writers say, he essentially brought into being the modern way of life. In *Empires of Light,* a book that tells how Tesla and others established long-distance electric power transmission in the United States, Jill Jonnes writes:

> Electricity unleashed the Second Industrial Revolution, bestowing on man incredible gifts: the untold hours once lost to simple darkness, the even greater hours lost to drudging human labor, and the consequent freeing and flourishing of the human mind and imagination. . . . The coming of electricity ultimately expanded the whole human sense of time, energy, and possibility.

That expansion could not have taken place without Nikola Tesla.

PROLIFIC GENIUS

If Tesla had invented nothing else besides his electrical distribution system and the motors it powered, he would still have had the honor of being one of the few individuals whose work profoundly changed the world. Speaking when awarding Tesla the American Institution of Electrical Engineers' Edison Medal in May 1918, Swiss-born electrical engineer Bernard A. Behrend (1875–1932) said:

> Were we to seize and eliminate from our industrial world the results of Mr. Tesla's work, the wheels of industry would cease to turn, our electric cars and trains would stop, our towns would be dark, our mills would be dead and idle. Yes, so far reaching is his work that it has become the warp and woof of industry.

In fact, however, Tesla was unbelievably prolific. Several years before Italian inventor Guglielmo Marconi (1874–1937), often called the father of radio, began to publish his experiments, Tesla designed and patented the basic pattern of circuits that underlies radio and television. Tesla also created the concepts and, to a varying extent, the technology behind dozens of other inventions that are now a part of the everyday world, from fluorescent lights and neon signs to radar, robots, and cell phones.

At the height of his fame, in the last years of the 19th century and the first years of the 20th, newspapers called Tesla one of the greatest inventors of his time. Four decades later, however, he died alone, in poverty, and all but forgotten. His rise and fall represent only one of the mysteries in the life of this strange, enigmatic man. How did he manage to have so many prophetic ideas, yet fail to develop any invention other than the electricity distribution system into a practical and financially rewarding form? Why was he able to sustain so few relationships, either in business or in his personal life? Was his genius marred by mental illness?

A TROUBLED LIFE

The answers to many of the puzzles in Nikola Tesla's life probably will never be known. This volume in the Trailblazers in Science and Technology set, however, outlines what biographers have discovered about Tesla and explores both his achievements and his failures.

Chapter 1 recounts Tesla's childhood and youth in what is now Croatia, including his first inventions and several illnesses that nearly killed him. It also describes his education in Austria, his invention of a new kind of electric motor, and his first major job as an electrical engineer, for which he moved to Paris in 1882.

Frustrated by his employers' lack of interest in his ideas, Tesla traveled to the United States to meet Thomas Alva Edison (1847–1931), the most famous inventor of his time, as chapter 2 explains. Edison, inventor of the phonograph and the first practical electric light, hired Tesla, but the two men were opposites in personality and in their approach to invention, and they soon parted company. For a few bleak months, Tesla was reduced to digging ditches for a living. In 1888, however, he gained the support of wealthy businessman-inventor George Westinghouse (1846–1914), who agreed with Tesla that the form of electricity called *alternating current (AC)*, in which the direction of the current's flow reverses many times each second, was the only practical one for distributing electric power over long distances.

Thomas Edison strongly disagreed. Edison had already established several power stations that produced electricity in the form of *direct current (DC)*, which has a steady flow, and he believed that only this form of electric power was safe. Chapter 3 describes the fierce competition between the Edison and the Tesla-Westinghouse systems, which reporters of the time called the "war of the currents," in the late 1880s and early 1890s. Tesla and Westinghouse ultimately won the war because AC could be transmitted over long distances, whereas DC could not. They displayed their triumph at the 1893 World's Fair in Chicago, whose spectacular lighting was powered by alternating current.

Chapter 4 tells how AC achieved an even greater victory in the mid-1890s when the Tesla-Westinghouse system harnessed the tremendous power of Niagara Falls to send electricity to nearby industries, the city of Buffalo (22 miles [35.4 km] from the falls), and, ultimately, New York City. Tesla himself, however, suffered a disastrous laboratory fire in 1895 and the first of many business reverses. Nonetheless, he began investigating worldwide transmission of signals and electrical power and produced the world's first remote-controlled machine, a miniature boat, which he demonstrated in 1898.

Chapter 5 begins by recounting Tesla's adventures in Colorado Springs, where he moved for eight eventful months in 1899. On one memorable occasion he burned out the power supply for the entire town, and on another he detected what he thought were signals from intelligent beings on another planet. The chapter also analyzes Tesla's rocky relationship with influential financier John Pierpont Morgan (1837–1913) and describes the giant tower that Tesla built on Long Island, which he hoped would be the start of his worldwide transmission empire.

Tesla's last years, marred by growing debt and poverty as one business venture after another failed, are the subject of chapter 6. This chapter explains that the mysteries surrounding Tesla's life continued after his death in 1943, when government officials seized his effects for unknown purposes. Tesla was all but forgotten when he died, but his fame was restored in later years, the end of the chapter points out. For instance, on June 21, 1943, just a few months after he died, the U.S. Supreme Court ruled in a patent case that Tesla, not Marconi, was the true creator of radio.

The conclusion lists several recent inventions that grew out of concepts Nikola Tesla was the first to describe. Not all of Tesla's dreams have been realized even today, but his work continues to inspire his spiritual descendants to explore the endless possibilities that nature and science present.

First Inventions

Nikola Tesla was surrounded by lightning from his birth. The eccentric inventor loved to tell people that he had been born exactly at midnight on the night of July 9–10, 1856, in the middle of a summer storm. A more fitting beginning for this pioneer in the science and technology of electricity could hardly be imagined.

AN UNEASY CHILDHOOD

Dramatic though Tesla's entry into life may have been, his family was humble. They lived in Smiljan, a village on a plateau between the Velebit Mountains and the eastern shore of the Adriatic Sea. This land lies in Croatia today, but when Tesla was born it was in a province called Lika, part of the Austrian Empire. Most people in the area belonged to a Slavic ethnic group called the Croats, but both of Tesla's parents were Serbs, members of a rival Slavic people. Tesla learned epic poems celebrating the deeds of Serbian folk heroes from his mother and enjoyed reciting them all his life.

Tesla's father, Milutin Tesla (1819–79), was the son of a military man and had been trained as an officer, but he left the army for the church. He was the minister of Smiljan during Nikola's childhood. In Tesla's autobiography, published as a series of articles in a magazine called *Electrical Experimenter* in 1919, the inventor wrote that his father "was a very erudite man" and trained him in memory, reasoning, and critical thinking.

1

Tesla believed that his talent for invention, on the other hand, came from his mother, the former Djouka Mandich (1822–92). Djouka Tesla could not read, but her proud son said that she invented a number of useful farm and household devices. She was also famous in the village for her beautiful needlework. "She was a truly great woman, of rare skill, courage and fortitude," Tesla wrote.

Tragedy overshadowed young Nikola's life. He was his family's fourth child and second son. (A fifth child, a daughter, was born later.) His older brother, Dane, was his parents' favorite. Everyone believed that Dane, seven years older than Nikola, was brilliant and would achieve great success when he grew up. When Nikola was about five years old, however, Dane died after falling from a horse.

Dane's death devastated the family. Tesla wrote in his autobiography that for many years, anything he did seemed to his parents to be merely a pale reflection of the genius his brother had been expected to show. Tesla himself felt his brother's loss keenly.

Nikola had his own close brushes with death during his childhood, his autobiography stated. He fell into a tank of hot milk, for instance, and was

Nikola Tesla was born in this small house in the village of Smiljan, now part of the country of Croatia in central Europe. *(Kenneth M. Swezey Papers, Archives Center, National Museum of American History, Smithsonian Institution)*

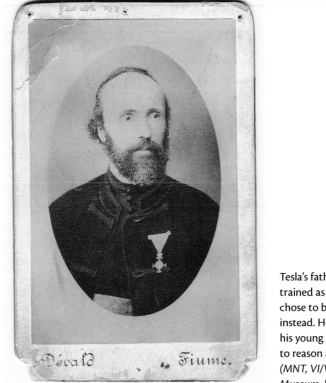

Tesla's father, Milutin Tesla, was trained as a military officer but chose to become a minister instead. He shared his library with his young son and taught him how to reason and think critically. *(MNT, VI/VI, 11, © Nikola Tesla Museum, Belgrade)*

pulled out just in time to escape drowning or being seriously burned. On another occasion, spurred by what was to become a lifelong dream of flying, he jumped off a barn roof while holding an umbrella as a makeshift parachute. The worn umbrella collapsed, and young Nikola landed hard on the ground. Tesla wrote that his inventiveness helped him survive his misadventures: "An inventor . . . is . . . better qualified than the average individual to protect himself in peril, for he is observant and resourceful."

MYSTERIOUS FORCE

Tesla's fascination with electricity began in early childhood. In the 1930s, when Tesla was an old man, he wrote in a letter to a child named Pola Fotić, the daughter of the Yugoslavian ambassador to the United States, that one winter when he was just three years old, the village experienced a cold snap during which the weather was drier than anyone could remember. The low humidity activated the phenomenon of *static electricity*, which makes objects and even living things accumulate an electric charge simply from the friction of moving. When the electricity discharged, it produced startling effects. "People walking in the snow left a luminous trail behind them, and a snowball thrown against an obstacle gave a flare of light," Tesla recalled.

Mačak, young Nikola's beloved cat, provided the strangest sight of all. As he stroked the cat's back, it became

> a sheet of light and my hand produced a shower of sparks loud enough to be heard all over the house. My father . . . remarked, "This is nothing but electricity, the same thing you see through the trees in a storm." My mother seemed alarmed. "Stop playing with the cat," she said. "He might start a fire." But I was thinking abstractedly. Is nature a gigantic cat? If so, who strokes its back? It can only be God, I concluded. . . .
>
> I cannot exaggerate the effect of this marvelous sight on my childish imagination. Day after day I have asked myself, "What is electricity?" and found no answer. Eighty years have gone by since that time and I still ask the same question, unable to answer it.

Tesla was by no means alone in his amazement. People had wondered about similar phenomena since at least the days of ancient Greece. Around 600 B.C., the Greek philosopher Thales (ca. 624–546 B.C.) wrote that if someone rubbed a piece of amber, the golden fossilized sap of prehistoric trees, the amber would attract certain objects to it just as a magnet does. Thales did not know it, but this behavior is also caused by static electricity.

The Greek word for amber is *elektron*. In the early 1600s, William Gilbert (1544–1603), physician to Queen Elizabeth I of England (1533–1603), borrowed this word to name the mysterious force that had been seen first in amber. He wrote that many hard substances could be "electrified"—that is, made to behave the way amber does—if they were rubbed. Scientists today know that an *electric current* is a flow of subatomic particles called *electrons*, which carry a negative charge. Rubbing produced such a flow in amber and some of the other materials Gilbert tested.

INVENTIVE BOY

Milutin Tesla's church promoted him, making him pastor of the nearby town of Gospić, and the Tesla family moved there when Nikola was six years old. The boy did not like town life at first, missing the closeness to nature that he had enjoyed in Smiljan. About a year later, however, his feelings improved when he briefly became the town hero. The Gospić fire department had just acquired a new water pump, and the firefighters took the pump to the river to demonstrate it. "The entire population [of the town] turned out to witness the great spectacle," Tesla wrote in his autobiography. When the firefighters began pumping, however, no water came out.

After this failure repeated itself several times, young Nikola had an inspiration. He wrote later that he knew nothing about the mechanism of pumps at that age but somehow sensed that the problem lay in the suction hose that led from the pump to the river. He waded into the stream, tracing the hose's path under the water, and found that the hose had become kinked, preventing water from flowing through it. As soon as he straightened the hose, water gushed out of the pump, drenching the surprised firefighters and the dignitaries standing nearby. In spite of this impromptu bath, everyone applauded Nikola. Some members of the audience lifted the dripping seven-year-old to their shoulders and carried him around the town.

Tesla's inventive side was also beginning to show itself. He made what was probably his first invention even before he left Smiljan, a little water wheel that had a design quite different from the usual ones in the village. Other water wheels had paddles, but Tesla's featured a smooth disk cut from a tree trunk. He cut a hole in the disk and pushed a straight tree branch through the hole. He supported the ends of the branch with two forked sticks, which he jammed in between rocks on the banks of a small stream. The lower part of the disk was under water, and the current of the stream made the disk turn. Decades later, Tesla would use this same basic design to make a new kind of engine.

In Gospić, when Nikola was about nine years old, he built an insect-powered motor. He glued two slivers of wood together in a cross shape and attached the center of the cross to a wooden rod, so that the rod would turn when the arms of the cross were pushed. The result looked like a miniature windmill, except that its blades were horizontal rather than vertical. With a thread he connected the rod on the windmill to a small wheel with a grooved rim, around which the thread also passed. The wheel, like the windmill, had a rod, or axle, running through its center and holding it in place. The grooved wheel, axle, and thread made up a simple machine called a pulley.

The young inventor then caught 16 large beetles, of a type called May bugs in Europe and June bugs in the United States, and glued four of them, all facing the same way, to each blade of his windmill. When the beetles tried to fly away, they spun the rod, which in turn made the wheel rotate. "They . . . continued whirling for hours," Tesla wrote. Nikola was very pleased with his invention until he showed it to a visiting boy—who calmly took a bug from a nearby jarful of spares and ate it! This sight so disgusted Nikola that he avoided insects for the rest of his life.

Young Nikola loved to read, borrowing numerous books from Milutin Tesla's well-stocked library. When he was about eight years old, he wrote later in his autobiography, he found a book that inspired him to begin to "practise self-control." This mental exercise soon became second nature to him, he claimed, and changed him from a weak and easily frightened child into one with an unbreakable will. He also developed his powers of observation, reasoning, and visualization. He became able to picture imaginary worlds in so much detail that they seemed as real to him as the one in which he lived.

Less useful sides of Tesla's unusual mental makeup also began to show during his childhood. Brilliant flashes of hallucinatory light frequently distracted him. He also developed a collection of unshakeable habits and fears, probably signs of what today would be called obsessive-compulsive disorder (OCD). For instance, he became fixed on the number three. If he performed an action more than once, he had to do it three times or some larger number that was divisible by three. As an adult, he would stay only in hotel rooms that had a 3 in their number or had numbers that could be divided by three. He also avoided women who wore earrings, especially round ones, though he had no problem with other kinds of jewelry. He hated touching people's hair.

STRANGE ILLNESSES

Nikola attended the Real Gymnasium in Gospić, the equivalent of today's middle school, beginning when he was 10 years old. He made high grades in mathematics, but poor performance in freehand drawing classes, which for some reason the school emphasized, dragged down his overall grade average. During these years he continued inventing, sometimes producing actual devices and at other times experimenting only in his mind. In his autobiography, Tesla bragged that these two procedures were the same to him: He could picture an invention in every detail, even down to wear and tear on its mechanical parts, and he claimed that when he finally built the machine, it always behaved exactly as he had thought it would. Some of the inventions he imagined at this time would become reality many years afterward. For instance, he saw a picture of Niagara Falls, the gigantic waterfall in New York, and told an uncle that one day he would use a huge wheel to make it produce electric power. About 30 years later, he made his vision come true.

In 1870, the year Nikola finished his studies at the Real Gymnasium, he suffered the first of several physical illnesses that beset his youth. For a time, he and his parents thought he might die. Tesla wrote in his autobiography that he was saved by the writings of American humorist Mark Twain (Samuel Clemens, 1835–1910), which made him laugh. Many years later, Tesla had the opportunity to tell this story to Twain himself. According to Tesla, the writer was so touched that he burst into tears.

After Nikola recovered from his mysterious sickness, his parents sent him to the Higher Real Gymnasium in nearby Karlovac (Karlstadt) to continue his education. He lived there with an aunt who was so concerned about his health that, ironically, she made it worse by allowing him very little food. He also suffered from malaria, a blood disease that he caught from the mosquitoes infesting the marshy city. In spite of these problems, he worked so hard at his studies that he finished four years' worth of course work in three years.

After Tesla finished his studies in Karlovac in 1873, he planned to return home, but his father told him to stay away. Tesla disobeyed this order and went back to Gospić anyway, only to discover that the town was in the grip of an epidemic of cholera, a highly contagious and potentially fatal digestive illness caused by bacteria. Tesla promptly caught the disease and, once again, nearly died.

Tesla by this time had decided that he wanted to become an engineer, but his father had been pressuring him to study for the ministry. As the young man lay on what both he and his parents believed might be his deathbed, he managed to gasp out (as he tells the story), "Perhaps I may get well if you will let me study engineering." Desperate to see his son recover, Milutin Tesla agreed. "You will go to the best technical institution in the world," he promised. Thus reassured, Nikola "came to life like another Lazarus," as he later wrote, and soon recovered completely.

Before Tesla could begin his college studies, however, another obstacle loomed: three years of compulsory military service. Supposedly to restore the young man's health, but probably also to help him avoid the draft, Tesla's father encouraged him to spend a year by himself in the mountains. Tesla did so, happy to be in a natural environment once more. During his year of wandering, he amused himself by designing fantastic inventions, such as a ring that would float around the Earth's equator and provide ultrafast travel from one part of the planet to another.

Several of Tesla's biographers say that Tesla's father, meanwhile, most likely had a quiet word with some of the high-ranking military officers in his and his wife's families, explaining that Nikola's health was too delicate for army life. Whatever the reason, the question of military service for Tesla never arose again.

UNDERSTANDING ELECTRICITY

In 1875, 19-year-old Nikola Tesla traveled to the Polytechnic Institute in Graz, now part of Austria, to study electrical engineering. During his first year, he

MICHAEL FARADAY'S GENERATOR: THE FIRST SOURCE OF STEADY ELECTRICITY

Scientists showed in the 1820s that an electric current produced a magnetic field around itself. Michael Faraday believed that the reverse was also true, but he could not prove it until 1831, when an accidental discovery during one of his experiments gave him a crucial clue. In this experiment, Faraday wound separate coils of wire, each sheathed with an *insulator* (a material that prevents the flow of electric current), around opposite sides of an iron ring. One coil was connected to a battery and switch, the other to a *galvanometer*, a device that measures current. When Faraday switched on the battery, sending current into the first coil, he knew that the electricity would create a magnetic field around the coil. He hoped that this field, in turn, would produce a current in the second coil, which the galvanometer would register. That did not happen—except very briefly, when Faraday switched the battery on or off. This told Faraday that a magnetic field could indeed create an electric current, but only when the field was moving or changing—being turned on and off, in this case.

Building on this discovery, Faraday created his first current generator or *dynamo*. It was a copper disc, mounted on an axle attached to a crank. By turning the crank, he could make the disc revolve. He set the disc between the north and south poles of a permanent magnet. He then attached a wire to one side of the axle and another wire to a piece of metal that rubbed against the rim of the disc. The two wires met in a galvanometer, completing a circuit. When Faraday turned the handle, the rotating disc changed or disturbed the field within the magnet. This moving field, in turn, generated a steady flow of electric current in the took about twice as many courses as he was required to do and excelled in all of them, but his parents greeted his achievements with surprising coolness. He learned later that the faculty had written to his father, warning that the young man's health might be at risk if he continued to study so hard.

Tesla took fewer courses in his second year at the institute, concentrating on physics, mechanics, and mathematics. During that year, his physics professor, a German named Poeschl, made a demonstration that opened Tesla's eyes to a new understanding of electricity.

circuit created by the two wires, which the galvanometer registered. Faraday wrote in his laboratory notebook, "Here therefore was demonstrated the production of a permanent current by ordinary magnets"—specifically, by a changing magnetic field. Expanding Faraday's basic discoveries about the relationship between magnetism and electricity, Nikola Tesla and others created ways to produce electricity at will and harness it for human use.

Faraday's Current Generator

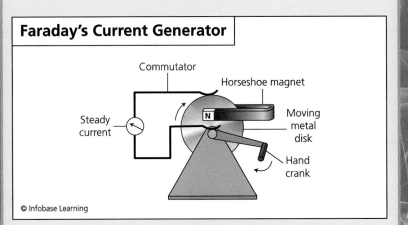

© Infobase Learning

This simple device, which British scientist and inventor Michael Faraday created in 1831, was the first to produce a steady electric current on demand. When Faraday turned the crank, it spun an axle in the center of a copper disc, making the disc rotate. The moving disc disturbed the magnetic field generated by the horseshoe magnet whose poles sat on either side of the disc. The constantly changing magnetic field, in turn, generated an electric current in the circuit of wires that ran from the axle on one side to a piece of metal attached to the rim of the disc on the other side (the commutator). The current continued to flow as long as Faraday kept turning the crank.

By this time, scientists had learned many things about this mysterious force. In a famous experiment in 1752 during which he flew a kite with a key attached during a rainstorm, U.S. scientist and statesman Benjamin Franklin (1706–90) demonstrated that lightning is a natural form of electricity. Luigi Galvani (1737–98), an Italian scientist, showed in 1781 that animal tissues respond to electricity. In 1807, British researcher Humphry Davy (1778–1829) discovered that chemical reactions can produce electricity and, in turn, an electric current passing through a chemical compound can break it down into the elements of which it is composed. Perhaps most important, several scientists in the 1820s had discovered that electricity and magnetism can be converted into one another and, in fact, are different forms of the same force.

Building on these fundamental discoveries, other researchers created devices with the potential to control electricity—producing current when needed, storing electric power, and using it to perform work. Alessandro Volta (1745–1827), another Italian scientist, made the first *battery,* an invention that could store electricity and deliver it as a continuous, steady current (as opposed to the sudden sparks of static electricity), in 1800. In 1831, Michael Faraday (1791–1867), a brilliant English chemist who began his career as Humphry Davy's assistant, invented the electric *generator,* sometimes called a dynamo, which uses a combination of motion and a magnetic field to produce an electric current. (Today, *dynamo* is used mainly to refer to a generator that produces direct current.) Electricity began to be put to practical use when Samuel F. B. Morse (1791–1872) perfected the telegraph in the late 1830s. Powered by electricity, the telegraph could send coded signals to receivers many miles away.

A REJECTED IMPROVEMENT

Professor Poeschl brought one of the latest electric inventions into his classroom in Graz. This *Gramme machine* was the invention of Zénobe-Théophile Gramme (1826–1901), a Belgian engineer working in Paris. It could act either as a dynamo, converting mechanical energy into electricity, or, conversely, as an electric motor, turning electricity into mechanical power. It was the first generator that could produce enough power to be useful on a commercial scale.

The Gramme machine consisted of a large, horseshoe-shaped magnet surrounding a hollow iron cylinder tightly wrapped with a coil of insulated wire. This coil-wrapped core was called an *armature.* When a steam engine or other mechanical power source turned the armature, the magnetic field *induced* an electric current in the moving coil. (Moving a coil in a stationary magnetic field had the same effect as keeping the coil still and moving or changing the magnetic field.) This current could then be transferred by wire to devices that needed electricity, such as the newly popular *arc lamps,* in which electric current jumping, or arcing, from one electrode to another through a gas created light. Running the process in reverse—that is, using a dynamo to feed electricity into the armature—turned the machine into a motor. The electricity made the armature rotate, and the armature, in turn, could be attached to another device by a rigid shaft and make that device move as well.

When acting as a dynamo, Gramme's machine generated electricity in the form of an alternating current (AC), which changes the direction of its flow many times a second. When the machine was used as a motor, brushes picked up the alternating current from a separate dynamo and transmitted it to a device called a *commutator,* which was part of the Gramme machine. The commutator, in turn, passed the current to the rotating armature. In the process, the commutator transformed the alternating current into direct current (DC), which flows in only one direction, by changing the direction of the alternating current's flow each time the current began to reverse itself.

The brushes and commutator frequently gave off sparks, an annoying feature. Tesla startled the class by suggesting that the motor be run on alternating current instead of direct current, which would allow the commutator to be removed from the device. Poeschl devoted an entire lecture to ridiculing this idea, for instance by showing that if he disconnected the commutator, the machine could no longer generate current. "Mr. Tesla may accomplish great things, but he certainly never will do this," the physics professor told his students, according to Tesla's autobiography. "It would be equivalent to converting a steadily pulling force, like that of gravity, into a rotary effort. It is a perpetual motion scheme, an impossible idea." In spite of this criticism, Tesla felt sure that he was right. He spent much of the remainder of the year trying to find a way to prove it, but he was unsuccessful, and he wrote later, "almost came to the conclusion that the problem was insolvable."

CONQUERING AN ADDICTION

While at Graz, Tesla became an expert at cards, billiards, and chess and developed the disturbing habit of gambling on the outcome of matches in which he took part. If he won, he generously returned his winnings to the losers—but he did not always win. In his third year at the university, he lost all the money that his father had given him to pay for his tuition at the University of Prague (now the capital of the Czech Republic) the following year. When he confessed this disaster to his mother, she gave him enough money to replace what he had spent. According to Tesla's autobiography, she said resignedly, "Go and enjoy yourself. The sooner you lose all we possess the better it will be. I know that you will get over it."

Tesla turned to his cards once more and, blessed with better luck, won enough money to repay his mother. He then applied his enormous self-discipline to cure himself of his gambling addiction. "I not only vanquished it but tore it from my heart so as not to leave even a trace of desire," his auto-biography stated. "Ever since that time I have been as indifferent to any form of gambling as to picking teeth."

In spite of his success at the card table, Tesla had to leave Graz before the end of his third year, probably because of a shortage of funds. He therefore never earned a degree. He spent the next year in the nearby town of Maribor, working to earn the rest of the money he would need in Prague. He went to the university in 1880, attending lectures on mathematics and physics for a few months. Then, however, his father died, and he realized that he would have to leave the university and look for paying work.

Tesla learned that Ferenc Puskas, a family friend, was about to establish a telephone exchange in Budapest, Hungary, so he went to Budapest in January 1881 in the hope of obtaining a job with the exchange. When he arrived, however, he found that the exchange had not yet been set up. (The telephone was still a new invention—Alexander Graham Bell [1847–1922] had patented it only five years earlier—and its infrastructure was not well established.) Instead, he found work with the Hungarian government's central telegraph office. Hired first as a draftsman, at a salary so low that he said in his autobi-ography he was ashamed to mention it, he was rapidly promoted when his superiors saw what fine work he did.

Puskas finally opened the telephone exchange later in 1881, and he gave Tesla the job of running it. Tesla invented several improvements for the com-pany, including a repeater/amplifier device that was an ancestor of today's loudspeaker, but he did not bother to take out patents on them.

THE AC INDUCTION MOTOR

Tesla's work at the telephone exchange was soon interrupted by another strange illness. His senses had always been unusually acute, but now, he wrote in his autobiography, they became almost supernaturally sensitive:

I could hear the ticking of a watch with three rooms between me and the time-piece. A fly alighting on a table in the room would cause a dull thud in my ear. . . . The ground under my feet trembled continuously. I had to support my bed on rubber cushions to get any rest at all. . . . In the dark I had the sense of a bat and could detect the presence of an object at a distance of twelve feet by a peculiar creepy sensation on the forehead. . . . A renowned physician . . . pronounced my malady unique and incurable.

Tesla recovered from his sickness in early 1882 and began to venture out into the world once more. While walking in a local park one evening in February with Anital (Anthony) Szigeti, a friend who had helped him through his illness, the 24-year-old inventor witnessed a beautiful sunset that made him think of lines from Johann Wolfgang von Goethe's (1739–1842) verse play *Faust*. Translated into English, they would read:

The glow retreats, done is the day of toil;
It yonder hastes, new fields of life exploring;
Ah, that no wing can lift me from the soil
Upon its track to follow, follow soaring!

Suddenly, as if the sunset and Goethe's poetry had inspired him, Tesla realized "like a flash of lightning," as he later put it, that he had the answer to the problem that had haunted him since his days in Graz: the way to build an alternating-current motor. He picked up a nearby stick and began to draw a picture of the device in the dirt at his feet. His diagram showed not only the motor but the rotating magnetic field that drove it—both completely new concepts. "See my motor here; watch me reverse it," he told the startled Szigeti.

Earlier attempts to build AC motors had failed because the inventors used a single circuit to transmit the current, just as was done in direct-current motors. Each time the current reversed its direction, it reversed the north and south poles of the motor's magnetic field as well. The motor therefore vibrated but did not turn. Tesla had the inspiration of using two or more circuits that were out of phase with each other. Coils embedded in the outer part of the motor, which did not move (and was therefore called a *stator*), formed the circuits, which obtained their power from a source of alternating-current electricity. The magnetic field generated by one circuit turned the armature (also called a *rotor* in this type of motor) a little distance and then began to reverse itself, but just at that instant the field of the second

Tesla's Induction Motor

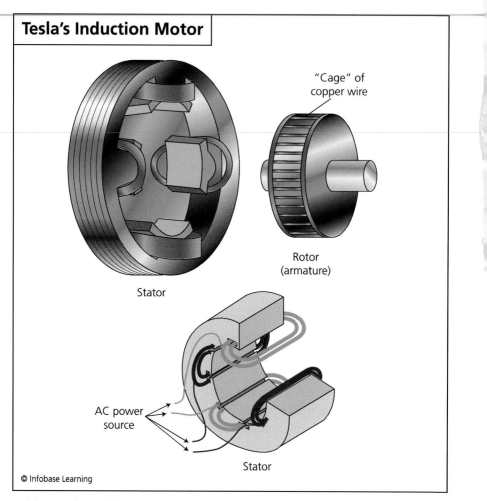

"Cage" of copper wire

Rotor (armature)

Stator

AC power source

Stator

© Infobase Learning

Tesla's motor depended on two or more electric circuits that were out of phase with one another and therefore generated a rotating magnetic field, which turned the moving part of the motor. The wires that make up the circuits are embedded in the stator, the part of the motor that does not move. In a two-phase motor, like the one shown here, the two circuits (one in red and one in green in the diagram) are 90° apart. The rotating magnetic field produced by the circuits turns the rotor, or moving part of the motor, and generates a current in the rotor (which is also the motor's armature) by induction.

circuit, which had been reversed, flipped into the forward direction and pushed the armature a little farther. The combination of the two opposing circuits created a magnetic field that, in effect, rotated—a "magnetic whirlwind," as John J. O'Neill (1889–1953) called it in his biography *Prodigal Genius: The Life of Nikola Tesla.* The whirling field dragged the rotor along with it, making it turn, and created an electric current in the wires the rotor contained as well. Tesla's motor was a type called an *induction motor* because power (both mechanical and electric) was induced in the armature by the magnetic field rather than transferred by physical contacts (commutators), as in DC motors.

Feverish with excitement, Tesla spent the next two months imagining one variation on his basic motor after another. They included the *polyphase motor,* which used three or more currents, all out of phase with each other, rather than the two he had originally imagined. As always, the devices were so clear in his mind that he felt no need to actually build or test them. He worked out not merely motors but an entire system for generating, transmitting, and using alternating-current electricity.

YOUNG MAN IN PARIS

Tesla's run of creativity was interrupted when Ferenc Puskas sold the Budapest telephone exchange, leaving the young man without a job. Fortunately for Tesla, Puskas's brother, Tivadar (Theodore) (1844–93), was a partner in the Continental Edison Company, a business licensed to develop the products of famed U.S. inventor Thomas Alva Edison in Europe. Tivadar introduced Tesla to Charles Batchelor (1845–1910), the head of the Edison factory in Ivry, a suburb of Paris, and Batchelor agreed to hire him. Tesla moved to Paris in fall 1882.

A tall, slender, rather handsome young man in (for once) the prime of health, Tesla enjoyed his first months in the famous City of Light. He swam in the River Seine every morning, then walked for an hour to reach the factory, where he worked on Edison's direct-current dynamos and motors and the U.S. inventor's new electric lights. In the evenings, he ate at cafes and talked with others who shared his interest in electricity.

Like Tesla's supervisors in Budapest, his superiors in the Edison company recognized his engineering talents and quickly promoted him. They were pleased when he invented improvements for their dynamos and regulators. When he tried to interest them in his new motor, however, they turned away. Edison believed that only direct current should be used, and they followed his lead.

The Edison company sent Tesla to different sites in France and Germany to act as a troubleshooter, solving problems that developed with their devices. Early in 1883, for instance, they dispatched him to Strasbourg, a city in Alsace (then part of Germany), after an embarrassing incident involving no

Tesla built the first model of his AC induction motor in Strasbourg in 1883. He created the model shown here about five years later, but the design was basically the same. *(SSPL/Getty Images)*

less than William I (1797–1888), the country's emperor. The company had installed lighting at Strasbourg's new railway station, but the wiring was defective, and in the middle of the opening ceremonies a short circuit blew out a wall, narrowly missing the elderly ruler. Not surprisingly, the German government refused to pay for the installation. The Edison company stood to lose both its reputation and a substantial amount of money if the lighting system was not repaired.

Tesla quickly cleared up the trouble, but convincing the German officials that the difficulty would not recur took considerably longer. While in Strasbourg, the young inventor found time to build his first actual motor, as well as a generator to produce the two-phase alternating current that the motor required. The city's mayor, M. Bauzin, tried to help Tesla find investors to help him produce the motor commercially, but he was unsuccessful.

Tesla returned to Paris in spring 1884, looking forward to collecting a large payment that the Edison company had promised him if he performed well in Strasbourg. Each of three executives he approached, however, referred him to another until, finally, the third man sent him back to the first one. The young man then realized that the supposed reward was simply "a castle in Spain," as he put it in his autobiography—in other words, a fantasy. This would not be the last time that a seemingly sure financial bonanza would elude Nikola Tesla's grasp.

A New Home

Charles Batchelor, the manager of the Continental Edison Company's factory in Ivry, was a longtime friend and coworker of Edison himself. Batchelor grew so impressed with Nikola Tesla that he urged Tesla to go to the United States and meet Edison in person. According to John O'Neill, he even wrote a glowing letter of recommendation for Tesla to give to the famous inventor. "I know two great men, and you are one of them," it read. "The other is this young man."

DIFFICULT JOURNEY

Frustrated by the unfair treatment the company had given him after his return from Strasbourg and hoping to interest Edison in his new motor, Tesla decided to take Batchelor's advice. In June 1884, he packed his few belongings and booked passage to New York.

The journey proved far more challenging than Tesla expected. Just as the train that would take him to his ship began to pull out of the Paris station, he discovered to his horror that his tickets and most of his money and luggage were missing, probably stolen. For a moment he debated what to do; then he extended his long legs and raced to catch the moving train. At the last minute, he grabbed a railing and hauled himself aboard. He found that he had just enough money left to pay the conductor for a new ticket.

Tesla's luck held—again, just barely—when he reached the steamship that was scheduled to carry him to the United States. He told the captain what had happened and even, according to the chapter about Tesla and Edison in Michael White's *Acid Tongues and Tranquil Dreamers: Tales of Bitter Rivalry That Fueled the Advancement of Science and Technology,* amazed the man by reciting the number of his lost ticket from memory. When no one else with that ticket number appeared, the captain let him board. Tesla's troubles were not over, however. During the trip, some of the crew mutinied against the captain and owners, and Tesla somehow became involved in the fight. He was not seriously injured, but he suffered scratches and bruises.

Tesla landed in New York with four cents in his pocket and very little else except the address of a friend who lived in the city and Batchelor's letter. He wrote in his autobiography that he found the new country "machined, rough and unattractive" compared to the "beautiful, artistic and fascinating" continent he had left behind. English was one of dozen or so languages he spoke, so he had no trouble communicating, but his first encounters did nothing to improve his opinion. A policeman whom he asked for directions answered him "with murder in his eyes," he later wrote.

Tesla doubted that he had enough money to pay for transportation to his friend's home. Fortunately, however, on his way he passed a shop whose owner was trying unsuccessfully to repair an electrical machine that did not work. Tesla offered to fix it, and the man gladly accepted. When the machine was running once more, he gave Tesla $20—as much as a highly skilled worker might earn in a week. For the moment, the young inventor's money crisis was solved.

DC VERSUS AC

Tesla found his friend and spent the night with him. The next day, armed with Batchelor's letter, he set out to meet the great Thomas Alva Edison. Edison by this time was world famous, known as the inventor of the phonograph and the electric lightbulb. He had begun wiring the homes of wealthy New Yorkers for electric lights in 1881, starting with that of John Pierpont Morgan (1837–1913), a powerful financier who would play important roles in the lives of both Edison and Tesla. At first, each house had its own direct-current generator to provide electricity for the lights. On September 4, 1882, however, Edison opened a central electricity generating station on Pearl Street to serve a number of buildings on nearby Wall Street, the city's financial center.

This model shows Thomas Edison's first direct-current electric power station, which he installed on Pearl Street, New York City, in 1882; it could serve only buildings that were less than about a mile away. *(William J. Hammer Collection, Archives Center, National Museum of American History, Smithsonian Institution)*

All of Edison's devices used direct current. The inventor was convinced that this form of electricity was the only one that was practical or safe. Much as Edison hated to admit it, however, DC had a severe disadvantage: It could be transmitted only a mile or so from its generator. Edison's electricity system would work, therefore, only if each building or small group of buildings had its own dynamo.

The reason for DC's limited range grows out of several facts about the nature of electric current. Current is made up of two features: the amount of the current, measured in *amperes,* and the pressure of the current, measured in *volts.* A current is a little like a river, with amperes describing how much water the river contains and volts telling how fast the water is flowing. The combination of these two—that is, amperes multiplied by volts—yields the amount of energy the current produces, which is measured in *watts.* (All these units are named after pioneers in the study of electricity, except for watts, which are named after James Watt [1736–1819], the inventor of the steam engine.) The amount of energy *(wattage)* tells, for instance, how powerful a motor the current can turn or how bright a light it can make. The wattage of a current can be increased by raising the amount of current *(amperage)*, the pressure of the current *(voltage)*, or both.

The amount of current an electrical system can produce for its users is also affected by the material through which the current must travel to reach them. No natural substance is a perfect *conductor* of electricity; all offer some *resistance* to the flow of an electric current. In overcoming this resistance, the current loses some of its energy because the energy is transformed into heat.

Different materials possess different amounts of resistance. Many metals are good conductors of electricity—that is, they have low resistance—and copper is one of the best. Edison therefore sent electric power from his generating stations to stores and homes through copper cables buried under the streets. Nonetheless, even with copper, the loss of energy to resistance was significant, and it was hard to reduce. Using thicker cables would have cut down on resistance, just as a wide pipe allows more water to flow through it. Copper was expensive, however, so Edison could not afford to lessen his resistance problem by carrying the current in thick cables. Resistance (and stress on the cables from the heat that the resistance generated) also increased if he added to the length of the cables or raised the amount of current (amperage) that he sent through them. Edison therefore could transmit only current of fairly low amperage, and he could not extend his cables very far.

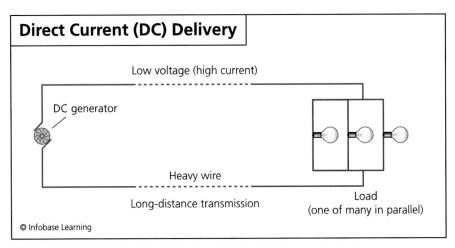

Direct Current (DC) Delivery

Low voltage (high current)

DC generator

Heavy wire

Long-distance transmission

Load
(one of many in parallel)

© Infobase Learning

One of the reasons why Edison's direct current could not travel far was that he could not change the voltage of the current. Increasing the amperage (amount of current) increased the energy loss from resistance, and increasing the thickness of the copper transmission cables raised the cost.

Raising the pressure of a current (voltage), another way to increase the amount of energy the current yields, does not increase resistance. Edison therefore had tried to make up for the loss of energy from resistance by having his generating stations send out electricity at a somewhat higher voltage than that at which lights and other machines worked best. Electricity loses voltage as it travels, and Edison had no way to raise or lower the voltage once the current left his dynamos. (Thick cables increase this loss, which is another reason why Edison could not use them.) This meant that the customers closest to the stations received power at a voltage higher than was useful, while those near the end of the transmission lines had electricity whose voltage was too low to make their lights shine at full brightness.

Transformer

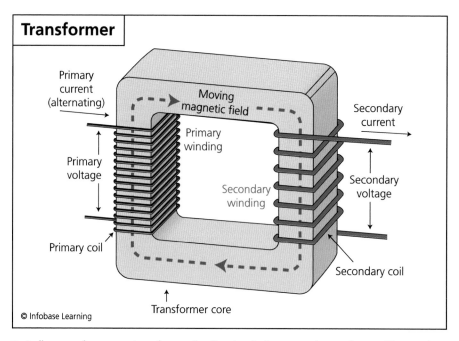

© Infobase Learning

Basically, a transformer consists of two coils of insulated wire wrapped around a core. The core is usually made of a material that transmits magnetism easily, such as iron. Electricity flowing through the primary coil (red) creates a magnetic field (green). Because this magnetic field must reverse itself rapidly, the incoming electricity is usually in the form of alternating current, which creates such a field naturally. The magnetic field, in turn, induces an electric current in the secondary coil (blue), with a voltage different from that in the primary coil. The greater the difference between the number of turns or windings in the primary coil and that in the secondary coil, the greater the difference in voltage will be. Because the secondary coil in the transformer shown here has fewer windings than the primary coil, this transformer is a step-down transformer—one that produces a current with voltage lower than that of the current entering it. If the secondary coil had more turns than the primary, the transformer would increase, or step up, the voltage.

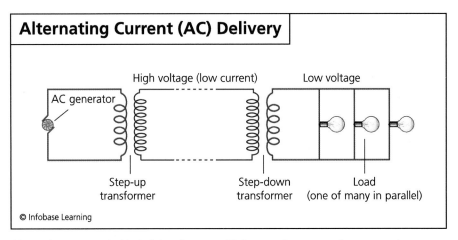

Alternating Current (AC) Delivery

High voltage (low current)   Low voltage

AC generator

Step-up
transformer

Step-down
transformer

Load
(one of many in parallel)

© Infobase Learning

Alternating current, the kind of electric current Tesla wanted to use, can be sent over long distances because transformers can raise and lower its voltage. A step-up transformer near the generator raises the voltage, allowing the current to be transmitted with a minimum of energy loss from resistance. A step-down transmitter near the current's destination lowers the voltage to a level suitable for use by homes and businesses.

Tesla's system, in contrast to Edison's, included a device that could solve this problem—but it worked only with alternating current. Called a *transformer,* it used the effects of a magnetic field to raise or lower the voltage of an electric current. It required alternating current because only AC's rapidly changing flow could produce the varying magnetic field that the transformer needed. (Transformers that work with DC can be made today, but they did not exist in Tesla's time.) Tesla did not invent transformers, but he was one of the first to see that they could make long-distance transmission of electric current possible. A transformer near a generating station raises the voltage of the current tremendously and reduces the amperage by a proportionate amount, keeping the total amount of energy transmitted the same but greatly lowering the loss from resistance. Just before the current arrives at the houses or businesses that use it, it passes through another transformer that reverses the process, producing the low voltage at which lights and appliances run best.

CONFLICTING PERSONALITIES

Direct current might have its disadvantages, but Thomas Edison had invested a great deal of effort and money in his DC system and had no interest in hearing Nikola Tesla explain why he should use a completely different one.

Edison also apparently was not sure what to make of the young man himself. Probably thinking of the fictional vampire Dracula, who was said to have lived in roughly the same part of Europe as Tesla, Edison (according to an article in the February 1894 *Century* magazine) startled Tesla during their interview by asking him whether he had ever tasted human flesh! Nonethe-

THOMAS ALVA EDISON (1847–1931): THE WIZARD OF MENLO PARK

Born in Milan, Ohio, on February 11, 1847, Thomas Edison grew up in Port Huron, Michigan. He did poorly in school for three months, so his mother taught him at home. As a young man he became a telegraph operator, a job that introduced him to electricity. It also inspired his first inventions, including an automatic repeater that sent signals between unmanned telegraph stations, an electric vote recorder (for which he earned his first patent, in 1869), and a stock ticker.

Edison went on to develop a series of inventions that became mainstays of 20th-century life, including the phonograph (1877), the most commercially successful form of incandescent lamp (early 1880s), a generation and distribution system for direct-current electricity (1882), and motion pictures (1888). He also created improved forms of the telegraph, telephone, electric dynamo, storage battery, DC electric motor, and many more inventions of others. He earned almost 1,100 patents in the United States alone, as well as a number in European countries, during his lifetime.

One of Edison's most important inventions was not a device but a way of inventing: the technological or industrial research laboratory. He founded his first one in Menlo Park, New Jersey, in 1876. In essence, he applied to invention the same principle that his contemporary Henry Ford (1863–1947) was using to manufacture automobiles: mass production. Edison once said that he intended his facility to develop "a minor invention every ten days and a big thing every six months or so."

Edison and Tesla each criticized the other's style of inventing. After Edison passed away on October 18, 1931, Tesla commented:

> If he had a needle to find in a haystack he would not stop to reason where it was most likely to be, but would proceed at once

less, impressed either by Batchelor's praise or by some quality in Tesla himself, Edison hired him as an engineer.

Tesla had a chance to win Edison's favor a few weeks later, he wrote in his autobiography. The lights on the ocean liner S.S. *Oregon*, the country's fastest passenger steamship and the first to have electric lighting, had failed, and

with the feverish diligence of a bee, to examine straw after straw until he found the object of his search. . . . Just a little theory and calculation would have saved him 90 per cent of the labor.

Edison, for his part, once complained that "Tesla is a man who is always going to do something"—that is, Tesla loved to talk about how successful his inventions would be but seldom achieved what he promised. Nonetheless, Edison said near the end of his life that his greatest mistake had been his failure to recognize Tesla's genius when he had the chance.

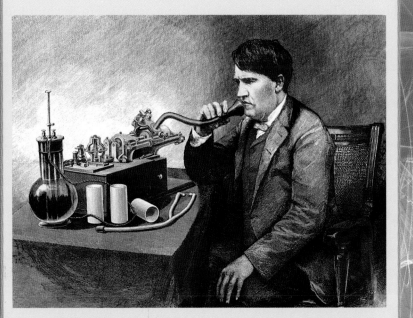

Thomas Edison, shown here speaking through his phonograph in the 1870s, was one of the most prolific inventors of all time. Unlike Tesla, who preferred working alone, Edison employed large numbers of people to help him develop and commercialize his inventions. (© *North Wind Picture Archives/Alamy*)

the ship's dynamos were too large to be removed from its hold and taken back to the Edison factory for repairs. Without functioning lights, the *Oregon* could not sail, and its departure was well overdue. Edison sent Tesla to fix the problem.

Aided by the ship's crew, the young engineer worked on the ailing dynamos all night and finally completed the repair around dawn. As he was returning to the office, he met Edison, on his own way home with Batchelor (recently returned from Paris) and a few other friends. (One thing Tesla and Edison had in common was an ability to function with very little sleep.) "Here is our Parisian, running around at night," Edison said. Tesla told him that the lights on the *Oregon* were functioning once again. Edison said nothing to him, but as he walked away, Tesla heard him remark to Batchelor, "This is a . . . [very] good man."

Tesla spent the next few months redesigning dynamos and other machines for Edison's company. He worked all day, every day, and most of the nights as well. "I have had many hardworking assistants but you take the cake," Edison told him, according to Tesla's autobiography.

Nonetheless, Tesla's employment at the Edison Machine Works did not end happily. Tesla claimed later that Edison promised to pay him $50,000 (more than $1 million in today's money) if he improved the design of the company's generators. After about a month of hard work, the young engineer completed the project. When he asked for the promised reward, however, Edison told him, "Tesla, you don't understand our American humor." The money offer, he said, had been merely a joke. Tesla must have felt that this was the Strasbourg story all over again, and he quit in disgust.

Tesla's biographers agree that he and Edison probably would not have worked together for long in any case because their personalities and approaches to invention were completely opposite. Tesla was a cultured, highly educated European; Edison prided himself on being mostly self-taught and despised academic learning. Tesla was always well dressed and careful about his appearance; Edison was sloppy. Tesla insisted on working alone or with only a single assistant, while Edison employed an army of other inventors to perfect his creations. Tesla's inexperience with financial matters and lack of concern for them allowed him to be cheated time and again during his career; Edison, on the other hand, was an excellent businessman. Perhaps the most important difference of all was that Edison "tinkered" with his inventions, improving them slowly by trial and error, whereas Tesla did all his experimenting in his mind, building actual machines only when his designs for them were complete. T. Commerford Martin (1856–1924), a well-known electrical engineer and magazine editor who knew both men, wrote later, "These two men are singularly representative of different kinds of training, different methods, and different strains."

SHAKY STARTS IN BUSINESS

By the time Nikola Tesla left the Edison company, his reputation as an engineer had started to spread. On March 30, 1885, he applied for his first patent, on an improved design for an arc lamp. A group of investors then approached him and offered to form a company around him, to be called Tesla Electric Light and Manufacturing. Tesla happily agreed, but he soon discovered that the investors were interested only in the arc lamp and cared nothing about his AC motor, which was far more important to him. A year later, after the arc lamp went into commercial production, the money men voted him out of the company. All he had to show for his work was a stock certificate, beautifully engraved but (since the company was new and unknown) worth almost nothing.

The year between spring 1886 and spring 1887 was probably the bleakest of Tesla's life. The highly cultured young man had to work as a ditch digger to survive. Even in the ditches, however, he continued to talk about his AC motor, and the foreman of the digging crew heard him. The foreman happened to be a friend of Alfred Brown, an engineer who worked for the Western Union Telegraph Company, and he introduced Tesla to Brown. Brown, in turn, liked Tesla's idea and put him in touch with another set of investors.

The investors formed the Tesla Electric Company in April 1887. Tesla, his ditch-digging days over forever, now had his own laboratory and a free hand to build the motors and other devices that he had worked out so carefully in his mind five years before. In return, he and the investors shared the rights to his patents. Within six months, he developed systems of machinery for single-phase, two-phase, and three-phase alternating currents. Each system included generators, transformers, electricity transmission systems, and motors, as well as devices to connect and control these components. He experimented with four- and six-phase currents as well, and he worked out the mathematical theory underlying all of his systems. Tesla and his company filed seven patents that essentially covered the complete basic system for producing, delivering, and using alternating-current electricity near the end of 1887, and the patents were granted in early 1888.

In May 1887, Tesla met Thomas Commerford Martin, editor of the magazine *Electrical World*, who became his close friend and booster. Martin persuaded Tesla to begin writing articles about his inventions and published them in his magazine. The editor had many contacts in the new field of electrical engineering, and he made a point of introducing Tesla to others who might help him. One of these was William Anthony, a professor of engineering at Cornell University in Ithaca, New York. Anthony tested Tesla's two-phase motor for efficiency in early 1888 and found that it was as efficient as the best direct-current motors.

Martin also arranged for Tesla to speak before the American Institute of Electrical Engineers (AIEE). On May 16, 1888, Tesla gave the group what proved to be a landmark lecture, titled "A New System of Alternating Current Motors and Transformers." Tesla pointed out that "In reality, . . . all machines are alternate-current machines, the current appearing continuous only in the external circuit during their transit from generator to motor." He demonstrated his AC motor and showed why it was better than DC motors; for one thing, it could be reversed instantaneously. William Anthony also reported on his tests of Tesla's motor. The engineers at the meeting were greatly impressed. In *Prodigal Genius,* John J. O'Neill wrote, "Tesla's lecture, and the inventions and discoveries which he included in it, established him before the electrical engineering profession as the father of the whole field of alternating-current power systems, and the outstanding inventor in the electrical field."

WESTINGHOUSE

One of the men who attended Tesla's AIEE lecture was George Westinghouse (1846–1914), head of the Westinghouse Electric Company in Pittsburgh, Pennsylvania. Westinghouse, as famous for his business ability as for his engineering skill, had become wealthy by inventing an air brake for trains in 1869. He shared Tesla's conviction that alternating current was better than direct current for delivering and using electricity. He had set up an AC power station in Buffalo, New York, in November 1886, and by the end of 1887 he owned more than 30 such stations. He also invented an improved type of transformer, similar to those used today.

Westinghouse decided that Tesla's AC induction motor and polyphase system were exactly what he needed to complete his own ideas about the distribution and use of alternating current. He introduced himself to the young inventor and began negotiating to buy his patents.

Tesla went to Pittsburgh in late July 1888 to meet Westinghouse and work out the final terms for purchase of the patents. Unlike the case with Edison, Tesla and Westinghouse liked each other immediately. Westing-

Financier George Westinghouse was an inventor himself, which no doubt helped him appreciate Nikola Tesla and realize how important Tesla's ideas could be. He realized that Tesla's AC delivery system and motor were the perfect completion of the primitive AC systems he had already installed in a number of cities. (*Library of Congress*)

house offered Tesla and his company a large lump sum payment (Tesla's biographers disagree on exactly how much) and royalties of $2.50 for every horsepower of electricity that Tesla's system generated. In addition to selling the patents, Tesla agreed to spend a year in Pittsburgh as a consultant to help Westinghouse's engineers put his motors into production.

Tesla's time in Pittsburgh was not happy. Preferring to work alone rather than as part of a corporate team, the inventor did not get along as well with the Westinghouse engineers as he had with Westinghouse himself. The company's existing generators produced a higher *frequency* of current (measured in cycles per second) than that which Tesla believed was most efficient for running his motors. He and the engineers tried to adapt the motors to the 133-cycle current that the engineers were used to using, in the hope of avoiding expensive changes of equipment at the power stations, but—several years after Tesla left Pittsburgh—the engineers finally came to agree that Tesla's preferred 60 cycles worked better. (Sixty cycles is still the standard frequency for alternating current.)

Tesla returned to New York in late 1889, glad to be free once more to work on any research projects he chose. His mind was teeming with uncountable possibilities. As he said at the end of a May 1891 lecture to the American Institute of Electrical Engineers:

> The field [of electrical engineering] is wide and completely unexplored, and at every step a new truth is gleaned, a novel fact observed. . . . The possibilities for research are so vast that even the most reserved must feel sanguine of the future.

Revolutionary as Tesla knew his AC system to be, he believed that it was just the beginning of the wonderful things he would discover or invent.

The War of the Currents

Even before George Westinghouse bought the rights to Nikola Tesla's revolutionary alternating current system, Thomas Edison was preparing to make war against Westinghouse's all too rapidly growing AC empire. Edison genuinely felt that AC was not safe because of the high voltages it used, and he believed that people should be warned of this danger. He also recognized that Westinghouse and AC were formidable rivals to his electric power business. He hoped that stirring up concern about the safety of AC would keep Westinghouse's system from spreading.

Edison's motives might have been partly selfish, but his fears about AC were not entirely unreasonable. Spiderwebs of electric wires overhung New York City and other metropolises of the late 1880s, some left over from businesses that had failed and others actively carrying current. More than a few of the wires dangled down nearly to the level of passersby in the street, and some carried high-voltage alternating current to power the brilliant arc lights that illuminated the streets at night. Even experienced electrical linemen were sometimes electrocuted when they handled wires carelessly. Newspaper reports of two such deaths in spring 1888 made the public begin to worry about the safety of alternating current.

DUELING ACCUSATIONS

Edison fired the first shot in what reporters came to call the War of the Electric Currents in February 1888, when he issued an 84-page booklet bearing a scarlet cover emblazoned with the word "WARNING!" in large letters. The booklet contrasted alternating current with Edison's own direct current, which used low voltages and was transmitted by wires buried safely underground. "The wires at any part of the [DC] system, and even the poles of the generator itself, may be grasped by the naked hand without the slightest effect," the pamphlet claimed, according to Jill Jonnes's *Empires of Light,* a book that describes the Edison-Westinghouse war. Edison's booklet also stated that AC was uneconomical because, unlike DC, it could not work with motors. Edison apparently did not remember, or at least did not mention, that several years previously a young man named Nikola Tesla had shown him an invention that would solve this problem. Not surprisingly, the booklet also said nothing about the fact that AC, unlike DC, could be transmitted over long distances.

Even before this warning booklet appeared, chance placed a powerful weapon in Edison's hands. Alfred Southwick, a dentist in Buffalo, wrote Edison a letter in early November 1887. Southwick explained that he was a member of the New York State Death Commission, a committee the state had appointed to find a method of execution for people convicted of capital crimes that was more humane than hanging, the form of execution presently in use. Southwick had heard that electrocution provided a quick, sure, and painless death, but he wanted Edison's opinion on the matter. Edison replied that Southwick was correct—especially if the electricity came from one of the alternating-current generators manufactured by George Westinghouse.

Edison soon found another ally for his anti-AC campaign. On June 5, 1888, one Harold P. Brown (1869–1932) wrote a long letter to the editor of the New York *Evening Post,* stating that high-voltage alternating current was so dangerous—presenting "constant danger from sudden death"—that the state should outlaw the use of all AC above 300 volts. Brown was an engineer and electrical consultant, but according to Jill Jonnes's *Empires of Light,* he was not well known in the field. Nonetheless, the New York City Board of Electrical Control arranged a meeting only three days later to hear Brown's testimony about the dangers of AC.

The board wrote to George Westinghouse, asking for his comments on the charges. At first, Westinghouse ignored the group, just as he had ignored the tirades of Edison and Brown. In July, however—about the time he met Tesla and arranged to buy his patents—Westinghouse wrote a lengthy reply to the criticisms, which the board read at its next meeting on July 16. Westinghouse complained that the campaign against AC was a "method of attack . . . more unmanly, discreditable and untruthful than any competition which has ever come to my knowledge." If his competitors wanted to discuss safety, he said, he was happy to reply in kind. He pointed out that fires caused by direct current had destroyed central stations or other buildings, including a "large theater in Philadelphia," whereas Westinghouse installations had been involved in no such fires. The New York board also heard eight affidavits from electrical workers who had received serious shocks from alternating current but had survived without permanent damage. Westinghouse's attorneys raised questions about the electrical expertise and motives of Harold Brown (who was out of town at the time of the meeting) and demanded proof of his allegations against AC.

THE ELECTRIC CHAIR

Harold Brown later claimed that he had had no contact with Thomas Edison up to this time, but after the July Board of Electrical Control meeting he asked the famous inventor to loan him equipment with which to demonstrate the dangers of AC. Edison responded by offering him the full facilities of his new laboratory in West Orange, New Jersey.

On July 30, Brown staged a demonstration at Columbia College (now Columbia University) for the Board of Electrical Control and other electrical experts and reporters, during which he electrocuted a dog. He administered several jolts of direct current at increasing voltages to the animal, making it thrash and howl in pain, before applying a shot of alternating current—at a lower voltage—which instantly killed it. Several of the people attending the demonstration walked out in disgust.

In addition to protesting Brown's treatment of the unhappy dog, some reporters who described the demonstration said that Brown had proved nothing: The animal had probably been so weakened by the earlier shocks that killing it was easy. To answer this criticism, Brown publicly killed several more dogs a few days later, this time using only AC current at less than 300 volts. Two of the three dogs died within seconds, but the third survived for four painful minutes.

Even before the first of Brown's cruel sideshows took place, one important vote had been cast for the Edison camp. Shortly after the July Electrical Board meeting, the New York State legislature voted to use electrocution as its method of execution after January 1, 1889. The legislature then appointed a committee of the Medico-Legal Society to determine how this method should best be applied. The head of the committee, Dr. Frederick Peterson, helped Harold Brown with his dog experiments in Edison's laboratory.

Brown soon persuaded Peterson, who in turn helped to persuade his fellow committee members, that alternating current was best for this unpleasant job. During a demonstration at the West Orange laboratory on December 5, at which Edison himself was present, the two men executed a calf and a horse. That apparently was good enough for the committee members, who voted unanimously on December 12 to use alternating current in the state's executions. The following spring, the New York State prison system hired Brown to design the execution apparatus.

A test of the new method was not long in coming. On May 13, 1889, a New York judge sentenced a man named William Kemmler, convicted of hacking a woman to death with an axe, to be the first person to die by electrocution. The state began building the electric chair in which Kemmler would sit during the execution. Brown, working through intermediaries, acquired several Westinghouse generators to supply the current; he had to act secretly because Westinghouse would not have knowingly sold any machinery for that purpose.

Attorneys acting on behalf of Kemmler filed suit in a New York court, claiming that execution by electrocution was cruel and unusual punishment and therefore should be banned. Not only Brown but Edison himself testified that death by alternating current—which they proposed to call westinghousing—was sure and painless. (In *Acid Tongues and Tranquil Dreamers*, Michael White points out "the hypocrisy of attempting to claim AC was painless as a means of execution but caused horrible agonies if misused.") On October 12, the judge ruled that electrocution by alternating current was legally acceptable.

William Kemmler's execution on August 6, 1890, proved to be an ugly fiasco. Kemmler was at first declared dead after a brief shock of electricity, but he showed signs of reviving and had to be shocked again. The second shock was fatal—after two and a half minutes—but it clearly burned its victim as well as electrocuting him. This half-botched execution, the details of which appeared in newspapers all over the country, added to the growing public conviction that alternating current was too dangerous to use. Nonetheless, Edison and Brown were unsuccessful in their campaigns to have states outlaw high-voltage AC current.

THE TESLA COIL

Nikola Tesla took no part in the growing war between Edison and Westinghouse. After he left the Westinghouse firm in Pittsburgh in fall 1889, he went to Europe to see the Paris Exposition, brilliantly lit by both arc lights and Edison lamps and featuring the new Eiffel Tower. He also visited his family in Croatia. On his return, he set up his new laboratory and moved into the Astor House, a luxury hotel. (All his life, Tesla would prefer living in hotels to owning a house.) Young, handsome, famous, and wealthy, he began to make regular appearances in New York's high society.

As always, however, Tesla spent most of his time in his laboratory. His interest was now in devices that used high-frequency, high-voltage electric current. He already knew that high-voltage currents (if they were of low amperage) could be relatively safe, yet very powerful. Higher frequencies allowed energy to be transmitted more efficiently, with less loss along the way.

The prolific inventor developed one of his most famous creations, the *Tesla coil,* to supply himself with such currents. This device served two functions at once. First, it was a transformer, able to generate alternating currents with voltages much higher than those that came from standard transformers—up to millions of volts. It also acted as an *electrical oscillator,* a device that can "tune" circuits to generate current that alternates at particular frequencies. Tesla patented his coil in 1891.

The Tesla coil accumulated electric charge in a *capacitor* (or *condenser*), then sent the charge across a *spark gap* (two electrodes separated by air) into a primary coil. Only one of the two connections between the capacitor and the primary contained a spark gap; current flowed back and forth between capacitor and coil through the ungapped connection, creating pulses, or oscillations, that repeated many times a second.

A larger air gap separated the primary coil from a secondary coil; the air in this gap acted as the core of the transformer, substituting for the iron core of a standard transformer. The current in the primary coil induced a current in the secondary partly through magnetic induction (as in a standard transformer) and partly through a phenomenon called *resonance,* in which one object transfers energy to another without touching it (that is, it sends the energy through some medium, such as air or water) so that the two objects vibrate at the same frequency or at mathematically related frequencies called *harmonics.* By adjusting the sizes of the capacitor, the spark gap, and the primary and secondary coils, Tesla could tune his device to produce circuits that oscillated with any frequency he chose. He normally set the primary and secondary coils to the same frequency; that is, he tuned them to be in resonance with each other.

According to John O'Neill, earlier scientists had predicted the existence of electrical resonance, but Tesla was the first person to demonstrate it. Tesla

Tesla Coil

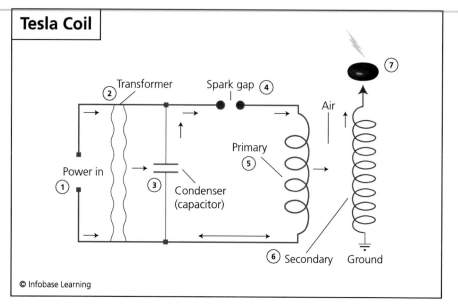

© Infobase Learning

A Tesla coil generates alternating current with very high voltages and frequencies. Power comes into the coil from a standard source of electricity (1). It passes through a step-up transformer, which increases its voltage (2). The charge accumulates in a capacitor, a device that stores electricity (3). The capacitor is connected to a spark gap, two electrodes separated by air (4). When the voltage in the capacitor becomes high enough, the accumulated current leaps across the space in the form of a spark. The current passes into a primary coil, more or less like that in a standard transformer (5). Some of the current flows back and forth between the coil and the capacitor, creating oscillations (changes of direction) that can repeat thousands of times each second. The device also has a secondary coil (6), separated from the primary by air that acts as the core of the transformer. The current in the primary coil creates a current in the secondary partly through induction and partly through resonance, in which a vibrating object makes another object vibrate at the same frequency without touching it. By adjusting the size of the spark gap, capacitor, and primary and secondary coils, Tesla could "tune" his device to produce currents with whatever frequencies and voltages he chose. He could also make the current accumulate in a holder on top of the secondary coil, which acts as a second capacitor (7). When this capacitor discharges, it can release gigantic sparks that resemble lightning.

also found ways to tune electrical circuits to respond (by resonance) to other circuits with a specific frequency even when the circuits were separated by a substantial distance, a discovery that laid the foundation for what would later be known as radio.

Tesla's device could produce voltages much higher than those that came from a standard transformer for two reasons. First, the secondary coil obtained part of its current through resonance, which *amplifies* signals, or makes them more powerful. Second, this coil could concentrate the voltage of its current as a *standing wave*. Tesla adjusted the length and turnings of the secondary so that as each pulse or wave of electricity reached the end of the coil and began traveling back the other way, it met and reinforced the wave behind it. The net effect was a wave that appeared to stand still, yet steadily grew in voltage because of the reinforcement. When the voltage became high enough—a million volts or more—sparks, sometimes of considerable size, flew from the top of the secondary coil.

A FATEFUL DECISION

While Tesla worked on his coil and other devices, economic fears were shaking the country in general and the two giant electrical companies in particular. The closure of several large banks in late 1890 began a nationwide financial panic. Both Edison and Westinghouse were in risky financial positions around this time, Jill Jonnes points out, because of their companies' very success: Their businesses were expanding rapidly, so both had had to borrow large amounts of money. When their creditors in turn needed funds, the creditors had the right to call in those loans with little notice. If the companies could not repay the loans, they would be in serious trouble.

Money problems had already forced Edison to reorganize his companies in summer 1889 into a new corporation called Edison General Electric. In February 1892, this company merged with one of its former chief rivals, the Thomson-Houston Electric Company, to form a new firm called simply General Electric (GE). Edison no longer had much voice in its operation. GE's real owner was J. Pierpont Morgan, who provided most of the money behind it.

George Westinghouse also found himself at high risk of losing control of his own company. When he asked financiers in New York for a loan to pay off some of his existing debts, they said they would grant it only if he let them make certain decisions about the way his business was run. One concession they demanded was that he free himself from his contract with Nikola Tesla, whose royalties on his AC patents could add up to a tremendous amount of money if his system was successful. Westinghouse did not want to break his agreement with Tesla, but the bankers were insistent. Westinghouse therefore visited Tesla in his laboratory in early 1891 and explained the situation. John J. O'Neill, who heard the story from Tesla himself, recorded the inventor's reply:

> "Mr. Westinghouse," said Tesla, drawing himself up to his full height of six
> feet two inches ... "you have been my friend, you believed in me when others

had no faith; . . . you supported me when even your own engineers lacked vision to see the big things ahead that you and I saw; you have stood by me as a friend. The benefits that will come to civilization from my polyphase system mean more to me than the money involved. Mr. Westinghouse, you will save your company so that you can develop my inventions. Here is your contract and here is my contract—I will tear both of them to pieces, . . . Is that sufficient?"

To put in perspective what Tesla gave up, Michael White points out that within a decade, the industrialized world was using millions of horsepower of electricity each month. If Tesla had received his promised royalties, even for a limited time, he "would have become the richest man in history."

Westinghouse still had struggles ahead of him—freeing the company from Tesla's royalties was only one of the changes he had to make—but on July 15, 1891, he persuaded the Westinghouse Electric Corporation's stockholders to sell enough of their stock to pay off the company's immediate debts. This made the bank loan unnecessary and let Westinghouse keep control of the corporation.

A WAVE OF SUCCESSES

George Westinghouse was soon able to demonstrate that the AC system he and Tesla had developed, including the previously uncooperative AC motor (now working nicely on the 60-cycle current that Tesla had recommended from the beginning), was ready to function in the real world. The Westinghouse Corporation installed the first commercial Tesla generator and motor at the Gold King Mine in Telluride, Colorado, in the summer of 1891, and both were a great success. The generator, powered by energy from a water wheel, produced electricity that was transmitted about three miles (4.8 km) up a mountain to the mine, where it was stepped down to power a 100-horsepower Tesla motor. Westinghouse engineer Charles Scott announced the success of this venture in an article in the *Electrical Engineer* magazine in June 1892.

Others were succeeding with the Tesla system as well. In August 1891, C. E. L. Brown and Mikhael von Dolivo-Dobrowolsky (1862–1919) successfully transmitted 190 horsepower of electricity from a waterfall in the German city of Lauffen to the International Electrical Exposition in Frankfurt, 112 miles (180 km) away. They transmitted 25,000 volts through the wires, then stepped them down at the exposition, achieving an amazing transmission efficiency of 74.5 percent. In *Wizard: The Life and Times of Nikola Tesla,*

Writer Mark Twain (Samuel Clemens) became a good friend of Tesla's and, along with other famous people, attended informal demonstrations in Tesla's laboratory. Twain is shown here holding a loop over a resonating Tesla coil while high-voltage current passes harmlessly through his body. *(Mary Evans Picture Library/Alamy)*

Marc J. Seifer writes, "Brown and Dobrowolsky had not only surpassed, by a factor of about one hundred, Edison's long-distance record; they had also transmitted significant amounts of power [as opposed to the relatively small amounts needed merely to run lightbulbs], a spectacular achievement with no comparable precedent." Dolivo-Dobrowolsky tried to take credit for the system, but Brown stated in the November 7, 1891, *Electrical World,* "The three phase current applied at Frankfurt is due to the labors of Mr. Tesla and will be found clearly specified in his patents."

Tesla himself, meanwhile, was having one of the best years of his life. He became a U.S. citizen on July 30, 1891, an attainment of which he was very proud. Furthermore, even without the Westinghouse royalties, he was an extremely wealthy man. Stories about him appeared in newspapers and magazines nearly every day. He had his own table at Delmonico's, probably the most famous and stylish restaurant in New York, and there he met the city's most powerful people, including his childhood hero, Mark Twain (Samuel Clemens), who became a good friend. After dinner, he often took his guests to his laboratory, where he provided spectacular demonstrations based on his discoveries.

LANDMARK LECTURES

Tesla's private shows were little more than elaborate parlor tricks, but he gave more serious demonstrations to his engineering colleagues. For instance, a talk to the American Institute of Electrical Engineers at Columbia College on May 20, 1891, featured a new "practical and efficient source of light"— bulbs that gave off a light as bright as that of Edison's incandescents but contained no filament and were not connected to any electrical wires. These bulbs contained gas that glowed in response to a high-frequency electric current that small Tesla coils nearby transmitted to them through the air. They were one of the ancestors of today's fluorescent and neon lights. Tesla's audience gave him a standing ovation, and the magazine *Electrical World* wrote that his speech was "one of the most brilliant and fascinating lectures that it has ever been our fortune to attend."

Tesla's fame extended far beyond the shores of North America. In February 1892, he went to London to deliver lectures to the Institution of Electrical Engineers and to the Royal Society, Britain's premier scientific organization. He then traveled to Paris to make a similar speech to the International Society of Engineers. In these lectures, he demonstrated not only his proto-fluorescent lights and Tesla coils but also a "carbon button lamp," which, according to several Tesla biographers, illustrated principles that would later be used in devices such as the point electron microscope, the laser, and the cyclotron or "atom smasher." He spoke about transmitting energy through the upper atmosphere, the Earth, or a combination of the two, an idea that would come to obsess him in later years.

The triumph of these talks was followed by a much sadder occasion. While Tesla was in Paris, he received a telegram saying that his mother was dying. He hurried to be with her, arriving at her bedside in Gospić just a few hours before she passed away. He returned to the United States in late August 1892.

THE BASICS OF RADIO

Tesla made another important lecture to the National Electric Light Association in St. Louis, Missouri, in spring 1893. In this talk, he made the first public demonstration of the basic technology that would underly radio communication: two pairs of circuits tuned to oscillate at the same frequency, which meant that they could respond to each other through resonance. His tools for his demonstration were two Tesla coils in which all four coils—that is, the primary and secondary coils within the two devices—were tuned to the same frequency. To each coil's secondary he attached a straight wire that went up to the ceiling. No wires connected the two devices, which were separated by 30 feet (9 m) of space. One Tesla coil acted as a *transmitter,* or sender of signals; the other was a *receiver.* In the receiver, Tesla had substituted an early type of fluorescent lamp called a Geissler tube for the usual spark gap. When he fed electric current into the transmitter, the Geissler tube in the receiver on the other side of the room glowed.

The secret of the wireless communication between transmitter and receiver lay in properties of electricity and magnetism that the Scottish physicist James Clerk Maxwell (1831–79) had discovered in 1864. Maxwell showed that combined electric and magnetic fields can travel through air or space as

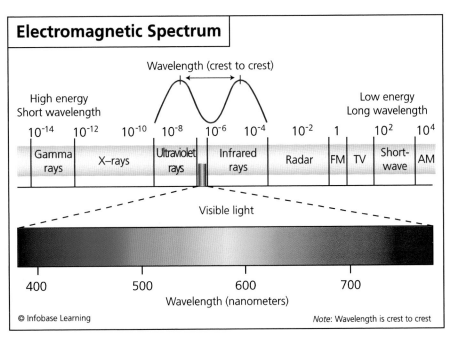

Electromagnetic energy or radiation, made up of combinations of electric and magnetic fields, exists in many forms. The forms differ in energy level, frequency, and wavelength. Gamma rays and X-rays have the highest frequencies and energy levels and the shortest wavelengths; certain radio waves have the lowest frequencies and energy levels and the longest wavelengths.

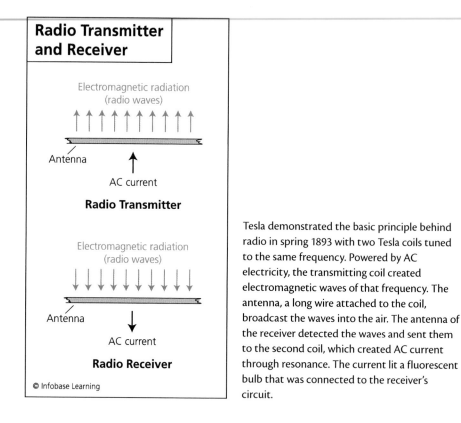

Radio Transmitter and Receiver

Electromagnetic radiation
(radio waves)

Antenna

AC current

Radio Transmitter

Electromagnetic radiation
(radio waves)

Antenna

AC current

Radio Receiver

© Infobase Learning

Tesla demonstrated the basic principle behind radio in spring 1893 with two Tesla coils tuned to the same frequency. Powered by AC electricity, the transmitting coil created electromagnetic waves of that frequency. The antenna, a long wire attached to the coil, broadcast the waves into the air. The antenna of the receiver detected the waves and sent them to the second coil, which created AC current through resonance. The current lit a fluorescent bulb that was connected to the receiver's circuit.

waves, moving at what was later called the speed of light: 186,000 miles (299,792 km) a second. Light is one of many types of *electromagnetic energy,* which together make up the *electromagnetic spectrum.* These kinds of energy differ only in the length of their waves, or, put another way, the frequency of their oscillation. *Radio waves,* the form of electromagnetic energy that Tesla and others would use to transmit signals, have frequencies below those of visible light.

Tesla was not the first person to send radio waves between a transmitter and a receiver. Heinrich Hertz (1857–94), a German physicist, had done so in the late 1880s. Hertz, however, had not been trying to establish a new form of long-distance communication; he simply wanted to prove and expand on Maxwell's theory. Tesla saw far greater possibilities in this phenomenon.

In Tesla's St. Louis demonstration, the long wires attached to his coils acted as *antennas,* devices that transform electric current into electromagnetic waves (radio waves in this case) or vice versa. The tuned antenna on the transmitter changed the electric current generated by the transmitter's coil into electromagnetic waves with a particular frequency of oscillation. These

TESLA AT THE COLUMBIAN EXPOSITION

During one week in August 1893, Nikola Tesla personally gave demonstrations in his exhibit area at the World's Columbian Exposition, also known as the Chicago World's Fair. Dressed elegantly in a swallowtailed tuxedo, he performed feats that any stage magician would have envied. Just as he had done for friends in his private laboratory demonstrations, he made

(continues)

Tesla amazed audiences at the World's Columbian Exposition with displays based on his discoveries. Here he juggles balls of electrical fire. (*Mary Evans Picture Library/Alamy*)

(continued)

metal balls spin on a velvet-draped table and filled the room with fiery discharges from his Tesla coils. Bulbs in the exhibit glowed without wires or spelled out the names of electrical pioneers in brilliant colors.

One reporter (whom Margaret Cheney quotes in her biography of Tesla, *Man out of Time*) wrote:

> Mr. Tesla has been seen receiving through his hands currents at a potential of more than 200,000 volts, vibrating a million times per second, and manifesting themselves in dazzling streams of light. . . . After such a striking test, . . . Mr. Tesla's body and clothing have continued for some time to emit fine glimmers or halos of splintered light.

John J. O'Neill explains that Tesla could survive such electric transmission because the amount of current (amperage) he used was very low, even though the voltage was high, so the current could not burn his tissues. The current's frequency was also high, which meant that its oscillations were too fast for human nerves to perceive and register as pain.

For most members of the crowd who watched the inventor, his demonstrations were merely one of many exciting shows that the fair offered. Few realized that they were seeing glimpses of the future—the forerunners of such common inventions as fluorescent lights and neon signs.

waves traveled through the air to the antenna of the receiver, which had been tuned to detect the same frequency of electromagnetic energy that the transmitter antenna produced. Resonance in the receiver coil magnified the signal. The receiver turned the electromagnetic waves back into alternating current, which lit the Geissler tube.

Tesla believed that the phenomenon he demonstrated could be used, not merely to send particular signals from a transmitter to a receiver, but as the basis of "the transmission of intelligible signals, or, perhaps, even power to any distance without the use of wires." He envisioned worldwide systems of message and energy transmission in which the Earth itself would be the conductor, the equivalent of his primary coil.

Tesla returned to his laboratory after the European and American lectures and continued to experiment, focusing on tuning circuits to be in resonance with each other. He tuned hundreds of coils to respond to different frequencies and showed that when he transmitted a particular frequency, current appeared only in the receivers that he had set to that frequency. He also demonstrated that, like the strings of musical instruments, his tuned coils responded not only to the frequency to which he had set them but also to harmonics of that frequency.

THE COLUMBIAN EXPOSITION

In 1892, George Westinghouse gained a great triumph that was a victory for Tesla as well. Chicago was planning to host the World's Fair, also called the Columbian Exposition because it celebrated the 400th anniversary of Christopher Columbus's discovery of North America, in 1893, and the fair's organizers wanted it to be illuminated by the new electric lights. (The fair was not held in 1892, which would have been the actual anniversary, because its planners did not want to compete with the presidential election that occurred in that year.) Both Westinghouse and General Electric tried to obtain the contract to provide the fair's outdoor lights, but Westinghouse made a considerably lower bid. "There is not much money [that is, profit] in the work at the figures I have made," Westinghouse told a reporter for the newspaper *Daily Interocean,* "but the advertisement will be a valuable one and I want it." On May 22, 1892, the organizers awarded the contract to him.

To provide electricity for the fair, Westinghouse's engineers built the largest AC power station in the United States. The station had to be able to supply current, not only for 160,000 lamps (the largest existing stations could power only about 10,000 lamps), but for a number of Tesla's AC motors as well. The 12 generators, which would be an exhibit in the fair's Hall of Machines, weighed 75 tons (68 metric tons) each. Westinghouse also planned to set up a working model of a complete Tesla AC distribution system, including two-phase alternating current generator, step-up and step-down transformers, a 30-foot (9-m)-long transmission circuit, and a polyphase motor.

The Columbian Exposition opened on May 1, 1893. During the six months of its life, it drew some 27 million visitors from around the world. It featured sights such as the first Ferris wheel, 250 feet (76 m) high and holding dozens of people in each of its cars. Exhibits from many countries were housed in the so-called White City, buildings of white stucco designed in the style of classical architecture that were built on canals and illuminated by many streetlights.

The Tesla-Westinghouse AC electrical system installed at the World's Columbian Exposition, powering some 160,000 lights, made the exposition a thing of beauty at night. This photo shows the Electrical Building, in which Tesla, Westinghouse, and Edison all had exhibits. *(Niday Picture Library/Alamy)*

As both Westinghouse and Tesla undoubtedly had hoped, "this fair showcased as nothing else ever had the new age of electricity," Jill Jonnes writes. The elevated railway that took people around the fair, the Ferris wheel, the boats on the canals, and most of the exhibits ran on electric power. Most spectacular of all was the Court of Honor, in which the largest buildings were located, when it was lit up at night. Jonnes describes it as follows:

> The sky darkened to a deep indigo. . . . Suddenly, the gold-domed Administration Building came brilliantly to pulsating electric life, provoking a profound sigh of pleasure from the crowd. Next, the long classic sweep of the peristyle on the far end of the Great Basin burst forth from twilight's shadow, wondrously luminous with the tens of thousands of Westinghouse "stopper" lamps glowing softly up in the cornices and along the pediment. . . . Next, all the white palaces glowed to electric life, . . . followed swiftly by the thousands of lights encircling the dark waters of the 1,500-foot [457-m] Great Basin, its rippling surface now a-shimmer. Hundreds of arc lights lining the walkways came on, spreading their blue-white coronas. . . . Ghostly gondolas and long electric craft looked like a fairy fleet. . . .

The people, who had never seen such concentrated, artistic electrical luminosity, let out a steady, breathless chorus of "Oh!" and "Ah!"

By the time the World's Fair closed at the end of October, the blazing lights of the White City had replaced the horrible image of the electric chair in most people's minds when they thought about alternating current. Even more important, the practical advantages of AC over DC were now clear to nearly everyone: AC could be carried over much longer distances, it was more versatile and powerful, and it was cheaper. The War of the Currents was over—and George Westinghouse and Nikola Tesla had won.

Waterfall of Power

The Columbian Exposition was not the only triumph that Nikola Tesla's system of AC power scored in the early 1890s. Through George Westinghouse, Tesla also fulfilled his childhood dream of harnessing the awesome energy of Niagara Falls. Tesla, Westinghouse, and others used some of that energy— estimated at between 4 and 9 million horsepower—to bring electricity, not only to industries built near the falls, but to the city of Buffalo, New York, about 22 miles (35.4 km) away.

HARNESSING NIAGARA

Plans to transform the mechanical energy of Niagara Falls into electric power had been made from time to time throughout the late 19th century, but little progress ensued until 1890, when a group of New York investors, including J. Pierpont Morgan, formed the Cataract Construction Company and placed a banker named Edward Dean Adams (1846–1931) at its head. Adams, in turn, established the International Niagara Commission in London and asked famous British physicist Sir William Thomson (Lord Kelvin, 1824–1907) to be in charge of it. The commission offered a $3,000 prize for the best plan to harness the falls, but neither Westinghouse nor General Electric entered the contest. George Westinghouse snorted that the commission was trying to obtain $100,000 worth of engineering ideas for $3,000. In fact, none of the 20 ideas submitted was deemed worthy of the prize.

In the early 1890s, a group of investors made plans to harness the tremendous mechanical energy of the water in Niagara Falls, shown here, to generate electricity. They decided to use the Tesla-Westinghouse AC system, a daring choice at the time, and gave Westinghouse the contract to build the powerhouse and generators. *(Andrej Glucks/Shutterstock)*

Adams and the other executives of the construction company then made a basic change in their plans: Instead of using waterwheels to generate electricity, as they had originally intended to do, they decided to use the power of the falling water to turn huge *turbines* (machines that use the force of a liquid or a gas to turn a central shaft) in central power stations. The turbines would rotate in a magnetic field, thereby generating electricity. The Cataract executives planned to start with just one power station containing three turbines and three generators, but ultimately they hoped to expand to two stations and produce 100,000 horsepower of electricity—an amount about equal to all the electricity being generated in the United States at the time.

Once contracts for work rather than mere prizes were being offered, both Westinghouse and GE submitted proposals. They sent separate bids for the powerhouse at the falls, the transmission line between Niagara and Buffalo, and the distribution system for electricity within Buffalo.

Both electricity firms—and, on May 6, 1893, just days after Chicago's White City had blazed into electrified life, the Cataract Construction Company as well—agreed that Tesla's polyphase alternating-current system should be used at Niagara. (If GE won the contract, it would have to purchase a license to use this patented system.) "This was, at the time, still a very bold and highly controversial" choice, Jill Jonnes writes in *Empires of Light,* since such a system had never been built on anything like this huge a scale. General Electric proposed to build a three-phase AC system, whereas Westinghouse planned to use a two-phase system.

On October 27, three days before the Columbian Exposition closed, the Niagara company awarded the powerhouse contract to George Westinghouse's firm. It gave the transmission and distribution contracts to General Electric, however.

A PEAK OF FAME

As Westinghouse's company began construction of the turbines and generators for the Niagara project in 1894, Nikola Tesla was at the height of his fame. His lectures in the United States and Europe had placed him at the top of the electrical engineering fraternity, and he won several academic honors that year, including the Elliott Cresson Gold Medal from the Franklin Institute and honorary doctorates from Columbia and Yale Universities. His display at the Columbian Exposition, meanwhile, had brought his name before the public as well.

Tesla's friend T. C. Martin continued to introduce him to powerful people in the media and New York society. Through Martin, for instance, Tesla met Robert Underwood Johnson (1853–1937), associate editor of *Century* magazine, and Johnson's wife, Katharine, both of whom became close lifelong friends. Martin himself wrote a long biographical piece about Tesla that was published in *Century* and also edited a collection of Tesla's writings, titled *The Inventions, Researches and Writings of Nikola Tesla.* Both of these, as well as numerous other newspaper and magazine articles devoted to the inventor, appeared in 1894 and spread Tesla's reputation even farther.

Tesla's combination of fame, apparent wealth, and good looks made him attractive to women, but it was an attraction he did not return. He enjoyed the company of Katharine Johnson and a few other women, but he never married or was romantically involved with anyone. And, despite rumors, no one has ever found convincing evidence that he was homo-

Nikola Tesla was handsome, seemingly wealthy, and at the height of this fame around the time this picture was taken in 1894. Women found him attractive, but he felt that a romantic relationship would use up energy that he preferred to save for his inventions, so he did not return their interest. *(Library of Congress)*

sexual. When reporters or friends asked him why he remained celibate—as they often did—he responded with statements like this one, quoted by John O'Neill:

I have planned to devote my whole life to my work and for that reason I am denied the love and companionship of a good woman. . . . An inventor has so intense a nature, with so much in it of wild, passionate quality that, in giving himself to a woman, he would give up everything, and so take everything from his chosen field.

"It is a pity, too," Tesla added. "Sometimes we feel so lonely."

DISASTER AND TRIUMPH

Tesla was not involved in the day-to-day development of the Niagara project, but the project indirectly had a major effect on his business life. Edward Dean Adams, the Cataract Company's head, visited the inventor's laboratory in 1894 and offered him $100,000 for a controlling interest in many of his newer patents. Tesla was happy to accept, because by this time he needed money badly. Part of George Westinghouse's advance payments had gone to support the young engineer's lavish lifestyle, but he had used most of the money to buy equipment for his growing laboratory. His experiments—especially those on wireless communication and energy transmission, which then interested him the most—could not proceed unless he found a new source of cash. In February 1895, Adams and other investors joined Tesla to establish a new business entity, the Nikola Tesla Company.

By this time, Tesla's experiments as well as his fame were reaching a peak. He was preparing to prove that his wireless system could transmit messages over significant distances, and he was beginning to investigate the Earth as a carrier of electrical energy. Marc Seifer writes, "He was sitting on at least a half-dozen entirely new inventions [such as the Tesla coil], each of which had the potential for creating completely new industries," although most of these were still little more than ideas that had poured from his fertile brain.

Then disaster struck. Early in the morning of March 13, 1895, a fire wiped out Tesla's Fifth Avenue laboratory, destroying his collection of model inventions and many irreplaceable notes and papers. (A night watchman, who escaped the blaze, said that the fire had begun on the ground floor, not in the laboratory, which was on the fourth floor.) Neither Tesla nor anyone else was hurt in the conflagration—the building had been essentially empty at the time—but the destruction was nonetheless devastating. "I am in too much grief to talk," Tesla told a *New York Times* reporter, according to Jill Jonnes. "Everything is gone. I must begin over again." A few writers recognized that the calamity was more than personal: Charles A. Dana, a reporter

Tesla, seen here in his laboratory, had many plans that were nearing completion when a disastrous fire destroyed the laboratory in March 1895. *(Mary Evans Picture Library/Alamy)*

for the *New York Sun,* wrote, "The destruction of Nikola Tesla's workshop . . . is a misfortune to the whole world."

The tragedy also came close to ruining Tesla and his new company financially, since Tesla had spent most of Adams's investment on equipment, and

The first Niagara Falls power station, shown here, went into operation on August 26, 1895, sending 15,000 horsepower of AC electricity to nearby factories. A little over a year later, it began transmitting power to the city of Buffalo, about 22 miles (35.4 km) away. *(Kenneth M. Swezey Papers, Archives Center, National Museum of American History, Smithsonian Institution)*

none of it was insured. Fortunately, Adams was willing to help the inventor recover, and with the banker's support, Tesla opened a new laboratory in July.

The Niagara project, meanwhile, was nearing completion. Its power station went into local operation on August 26, 1895. Delivering an unprecedented 15,000 horsepower of electricity, the station was, John O'Neill writes, "the most gigantic piece of electrical engineering conceived or accomplished up to that time." British novelist H. G. Wells (1866–1946) later called its turbines and generators "will made visible . . . clean, noiseless, starkly powerful."

The Niagara station first sent AC current to a number of industries that had built factories near the falls, the most important of which was the Pittsburgh Reduction Company, later known as the Aluminum Company of

CHAMPION OF RENEWABLE ENERGY

Unlike most engineers of his time, Nikola Tesla expressed concern for the environment and promoted renewable power sources. His most successful effort in this line was the use of *hydropower,* or water energy, to generate electricity at Niagara Falls. The Niagara installation was not the first to use water power to make electricity, but it was built on a far larger scale than any other hydropower plant of its day.

In 1898, Tesla told a newspaper he had created an engine that would operate on energy from the Sun. His solar powerhouse, he said, would be a large room with a glass roof. A huge cylinder made of thick glass, placed on a bed of asbestos and stone to prevent fires, would stand in the center of the room. A circle of mirrors would surround the cylinder, which was full of water. The mirrors would bend, or refract, the rays of sunlight entering the roof and send the light into the cylinder, where it would heat the water. The water, Tesla said, would be treated by a "secret chemical process" to make it warm more quickly than normal. The heated water would boil and produce steam that would spin standard steam turbines. Rotating in a magnetic field, the turbines would generate electricity. Batteries could store the electricity and dispense it on cloudy days. Tesla believed that sunlight would prove to be a far cheaper source of electrical energy than coal or wood.

Tesla published an article in *Everyday Science and Mechanics* in December 1931 in which he described two other types of power plant that would use renewable energy to generate electricity. One would employ *geothermal energy,* or heat energy from the interior of the Earth. Tesla proposed to sink a shaft deep into the ground and send water down into the shaft. The heat of the planet's interior would transform the liquid water into steam, which could be used to run a turbine. The steam would then be cooled until it became liquid again, after which it would be sent down the shaft to be heated once more. Other inventors had speculated about the possibility of using geothermal energy, but Tesla was one of the first to draw up detailed plans for a geothermal installation. Tesla's 1931 article also described a power plant that would obtain heat from the temperature difference between different layers of water in the ocean.

(continues)

(continued)

Tesla did not live to see solar, geothermal, or ocean energy plants, but later inventors developed these concepts further. Solar and geothermal power plants are in operation today, although they provide only a small share of the electricity used in the United States. So-called ocean thermal energy conversion (OTEC) plants have also been investigated experimentally, but this form of renewable energy has yet to become practical.

America, or simply Alcoa. This company needed tremendous amounts of electricity to extract the valuable metal aluminum from the clay in which it was embedded. A little over a year later, on November 16, 1896, the power station began transmitting electricity to the city of Buffalo as well.

The success of the Niagara project, perhaps more than anything else, convinced the country—and the world—that Nikola Tesla's polyphase AC system should become the standard one for producing and distributing electric power. Westinghouse soon installed seven more generators at the Niagara powerhouse, bringing its output to 50,000 horsepower, and GE later built a second powerhouse of equal size. The Niagara installation was eventually linked to the power system of New York City, about 300 miles (483 km) away. By 1902, the Niagara Falls power station was supplying a fifth of all the electricity used in the United States.

AN EMERGING RIVAL

At work in a fully functioning laboratory once more, Tesla continued to make great strides in 1896. His major interest was wireless transmission of signals and electric power, and during that year he filed numerous patents on inventions related to that subject. Most were for different types of oscillators that allowed transmitters and receivers to be tuned to particular electromagnetic frequencies. Tesla tested wireless radio transmission by having his laboratory send signals that he picked up on a receiver while traveling in a boat on the Hudson River, about 25 miles (40 km) away. He announced the success of this experiment, which John J. O'Neill calls "the birth of modern radio," in an interview published in the *Electrical Review* on July 9, 1897.

In addition, Tesla studied the form of electromagnetic energy now called *X-rays* at this time. The German physicist Wilhelm Roentgen (1845–1923) had discovered these rays at the end of the preceding year, 1895. According to John O'Neill, Tesla in fact had probably produced X-rays with some of his equipment several years before Roentgen did, but Tesla did not study the rays at that time or write any scientific papers about them, so Roentgen still deserved full credit for discovering them. Like Roentgen, Tesla made photographs with the rays (Tesla called his pictures shadowgraphs) and investigated their effects on fluorescent screens and other materials. Tesla correctly predicted that the rays would prove able to both improve and harm human health.

Tesla personally visited Niagara Falls in July 1896 to see his AC dream turned into reality. "It is all and more than I anticipated it would be," he told reporters afterward. "It is one of the wonders of the century." Soon after he returned from this trip, however, he heard for the first time about a rival who might challenge his more recent dream, to become the first person to achieve long-distance wireless transmission of messages or energy. An Italian inventor, Guglielmo Marconi (1874–1937), had demonstrated a wireless set in London earlier in the year. By July, he had transmitted messages through walls and over distances of about eight miles (13 km). Marconi applied for a patent on his system in England in December 1896.

Tesla's wireless plans were much more fully developed than Marconi's at this time. Marc Seifer writes that by 1897,

> Tesla had already conceived of a total plan for his world telegraphy system . . . that . . . utilized a variety of wireless modes, one being through the upper air strata, another by means of mechanical resonance, which he called telegeodynamics, and a third, and his most important, by riding terrestrial currents [natural low-frequency electric currents that move over large areas underground or in the sea, later called telluric currents].

Tesla filed the essential patents for generating, *modulating* (modifying), storing, transmitting, and receiving wireless signals in September 1897; they were granted in 1900. Tesla patented his inventions earlier than Marconi did, at least in the United States—but Marconi had the advantage that he publicized his demonstrations widely, whereas Tesla showed his devices only in lectures to professional audiences. Tesla refused to stage large-scale demonstrations of his system until he could perfect it and prove that it would work on a worldwide basis. Marconi's goals were much more modest, but he achieved them. He also made more rapid strides than Tesla in showing that wireless message transmission could be commercially practical.

ACCIDENTAL EARTHQUAKE

Some experiments that Tesla conducted around 1898 produced results so startling that they must have driven worries about Marconi completely out of his mind, at least for a while. They involved *mechanical oscillators,* which Tesla had invented in the early 1890s as a variation on the oscillators that he used to produce high-frequency alternating current. In this kind of oscillator, the primary and secondary coils are on a shaft attached to a piston. When powered by steam or compressed air, the piston moves the shaft up and down very rapidly between the poles of two electromagnets, making the oscillator produce an alternating current whose frequency depends on the speed of the motion. Electric clocks often use a device of this kind.

A mechanical oscillator can also be used in reverse; that is, electrical energy can drive the piston to produce mechanical energy. In this mode, the oscillator is essentially an engine with almost no moving parts. Unlike a standard engine, which changes reciprocating (back-and-forth) motion to rotary motion by means of a crankshaft, the oscillator produces only reciprocating motion. If its mechanical vibrations are set to resonate with and therefore amplify each other, they can have effects far greater than one would expect, just as the resonating oscillations in the Tesla coil can produce much higher voltages than those in a standard transformer. A troop of soldiers marching in step across a bridge provides a common example of mechanical oscillations that resonate and amplify one another; they can shake the bridge apart if their timing is right.

Tesla knew that as he tuned his oscillators to different frequencies, different objects in the laboratory responded to them. When he activated an electrical oscillator set to a given frequency, other coils in the laboratory, set to either the same frequency or one of its harmonics, sprouted crowns of sparks, even though they were not receiving current from a power source. Similarly, when he ran an oscillator in its mechanical mode and changed its frequency, different objects in the laboratory took turns shaking and rattling as the oscillator's frequency passed through the frequencies at which the objects resonated. The inventor did not realize, however, that these effects could extend outside the laboratory.

Tesla and his neighbors learned one day just how powerful the resonance triggered by his oscillators could be. His laboratory was on the upper floor of a building set among a mixture of factories and tenement houses packed with poor Italian and Chinese families, just a few doors away from the local police station. On that memorable occasion, the inventor attached a small mechanical oscillator—a mere seven inches (18 cm) long—to an iron support beam in the center of the laboratory and set it in motion. He did not realize that the beam was transmitting the oscillator's vibrations to the rest of his building and beyond.

John O'Neill describes what happened next, as the oscillator vibrated faster and faster:

> In an area of a dozen square city blocks, . . . there was a sudden roaring and shaking, shattering of panes of glass, breaking of steam, gas and water pipes. Pandemonium reigned as small objects danced around rooms, plaster descended from walls and ceilings, and pieces of machinery weighing tons were moved from their bolted anchorages and shifted to awkward spots in factory lofts.

In the police station, "Chairs moved across floors. . . . Objects on the officers' desks danced about and the desks themselves moved. . . . Chunks of plaster fell from the ceilings," O'Neill continues. The police, like the neighbors, knew all too well that unusual events in the area often could be traced to the laboratory of that strange young inventor, Nikola Tesla. As people in the neighborhood poured into the streets, therefore, several officers rushed up the stairs of Tesla's building and pounded on his door.

The officers opened the door just in time to see Tesla snatch up a heavy sledgehammer and smash it against a small device attached to a pillar in the laboratory—the oscillator. Feeling disturbing vibrations in the walls and floor, he had just guessed the danger, and he knew no other way to shut off the device quickly enough. O'Neill theorizes that the metal beam, which extended down to the laboratory building's foundations, had transmitted the oscillator's vibrations throughout the structure. The vibrations then moved into the ground around the building, which was made up chiefly of sand, an excellent transmitter of this kind of motion. When the sustained vibrations encountered buildings or other objects in the neighborhood that resonated with them, they produced effects like those of an earthquake.

In 1915, almost a decade after this event, Tesla told reporter Allan L. Benson (1871–1940) that with the right kind of oscillator he could split the Earth itself in half. He later admitted that destroying the planet might not actually be possible because the Earth would not show perfect mechanical

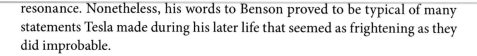
resonance. Nonetheless, his words to Benson proved to be typical of many statements Tesla made during his later life that seemed as frightening as they did improbable.

ROBOT BOAT

Tesla made one of his most important demonstrations at the Electrical Exposition in New York's Madison Square Garden in May 1898. It was an iron-hulled model boat, about four feet (1.2 m) long and three feet (0.9 m) high, which floated in a large tank. A thin metal rod rising out of the boat's center served as its antenna. The boat's interior contained a receiving set and motors that made the craft move. Tesla controlled it remotely by means of radio waves that he sent from a small, handheld transmitter, giving the boat what he called "a borrowed mind"—his own. He used signals with a variety of frequencies to make the boat start, stop, change direction, and turn its lights on and off.

People's understanding of Tesla's latest invention was colored by the fact that the United States was at war. A month before his demonstration, the U.S. government had declared war against Spain, blaming that country for the sinking of the battleship U.S.S. *Maine* in the harbor at Havana, Cuba, in February 1898 and for oppressing the people of Cuba, then a Spanish colony. After Tesla's demonstration, a college student asked him if a mechanism similar to that in his boat could be used to send missiles underwater to blow up Spanish ships by remote control. Tesla snapped back that the young man had missed the point: "You do not see there a wireless torpedo. You see there the first of a race of robots, mechanical men which will do the laborious work of the human race."

In fact, although Tesla was opposed to war on principle, he was proud of his naturalized citizenship and would have been happy for his invention to contribute to the war effort. He believed that it *could* be used to make a wireless torpedo—or torpedo boat, or submarine. When he tried to interest an official in the War Department in the device, however, the official proved even less perceptive than the student: According to an unpublished statement by Tesla quoted in John O'Neill's book, the man burst into laughter,

(opposite) This radio-controlled miniature boat, which Tesla demonstrated in May 1898, was both the first remote-controlled device and the first demonstration of a multichannel radio broadcasting system. *(Kenneth M. Swezey Papers, Archives Center, National Museum of American History, Smithsonian Institution)*

claiming that remotely controlled weapons would be completely impractical.

Both the student and the government official, probably along with most of the rest of Tesla's audience, failed to recognize that Tesla's *teleautomaton,* as he called it, illustrated not one but two major technological advances: It was both the first *robot,* or machine that moves on its own, and the first demonstration of a multichannel radio broadcasting system. "Tesla's teleautomaton remains one of the single most important technological triumphs of the modern age," Marc Seifer writes. "Here was a true work of genius."

Tesla, furthermore, believed that his invention contained the seeds of many more. He was convinced that in the future, teleautomatons could be developed to a point at which, essentially, they would make their own decisions and guide their own activities. He foresaw that his multichannel system, in which receivers were tuned to respond not merely to particular signal frequencies but to particular combinations of frequencies, would allow individual receivers to pick out only the messages meant for them from among the thousands broadcast from a central transmitting station and hear those messages in complete privacy. (He received a patent on this combined-frequency tuning in 1903.) Both of his predictions essentially have come true. Seifer points out that Tesla's teleautomaton and its control system provided the basis not only of radio and robotics, but also of other creations such as the cell phone, the garage door opener, the fax machine, and the cable-television scrambler.

NEW PLANS

Tesla could control his robot boat, but he was less successful in managing his financial destiny. As always, he needed more money for equipment and laboratory supplies, but he found that neither George Westinghouse nor Edward Dean Adams was willing to supply it. He also appealed to John Jacob Astor IV (1864–1912), another extremely wealthy man, to whom Adams had referred him. When Tesla and Astor finally met in person in December 1898, Astor said he was interested in helping the inventor—but only up to a point. Tesla had hoped that Astor would fund his research on wireless transmission, but Astor replied that he first wanted to focus on Tesla's oscillators and cold (fluorescent) lights. If Tesla could develop those inventions well enough for them to be produced commercially, Astor said, he might consider other projects.

Tesla agreed to accept Astor's terms. On January 10, 1899, therefore, Astor gave Tesla $100,000 in exchange for 500 shares of stock in the Tesla

Tesla lived in this New York luxury hotel, the Waldorf-Astoria (shown here around the time he moved in in 1899), for about 15 years, much of the time on credit because his finances could not keep up with his lifestyle. *(Library of Congress)*

Electric Company. Astor also became chairman of the company's board. As part of the arrangement, Tesla moved into Astor's new luxury hotel, the Waldorf-Astoria.

Regardless of his promises to Astor, Tesla continued to develop his own plans. Remembering his terrible 1895 laboratory fire and perhaps the "earthquake" incident as well, he decided that his experiments had grown too big for his New York laboratory to house safely. Only in a laboratory in the open countryside, he felt, could he build coils and other apparatus large enough to achieve his dual goal of sending messages and power wirelessly around—and through—the Earth for great distances.

Tesla had already visited a possible site in February 1896: Colorado Springs, Colorado, not far from the famous mountain called Pike's Peak. In early 1899, he contacted Leonard Curtis, a patent attorney who had helped him and Westinghouse protect his AC patents—and, more important for his present purposes, the head of the Colorado Springs Electric Company. "My coils are producing 4 million volts—sparks jumping from walls to ceilings are a fire hazard," he wrote to Curtis. "I must have electrical power, water, and my own laboratory. . . . My work will be done late at night when the power load will be least."

Curtis's reply was everything Tesla could have hoped for: "All things arranged, land will be free. You will live at the Alta Vista Hotel. I have interest in the City Power Plant so electricity is free to you." Tesla planned to use Astor's money to build a laboratory on the land that Curtis promised to provide. In May 1899, the inventor decided that the time for him to move west had come.

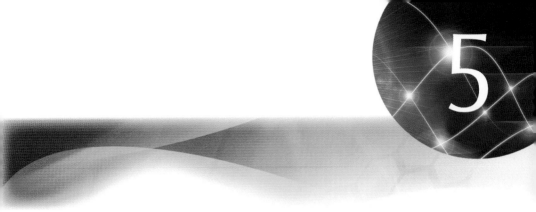

Towers of Dreams

Nikola Tesla arrived in Colorado Springs on May 18, 1899. The city administration welcomed him with a banquet. Many of the town's residents already knew his name because of his AC system's success in Telluride and other mining camps.

MYSTERIOUS LABORATORY

Tesla supervised the construction of his new laboratory, a barnlike structure about 100 feet (30.5 m) on a side, on land about a mile (1.6 km) east of town during June. Wanting to discourage curious citizens, he erected a heavy fence around the building with a sign that read, "KEEP OUT—GREAT DANGER."

The laboratory contained a large standard transformer, numerous receiving stations, and an assortment of small Tesla coils and other electrical equipment. Its most striking feature was a giant Tesla coil, about 50 feet (15 m) across and nine feet (2.7 m) high. The coil's secondary, some 75 turns of wire wound around a cylindrical wooden framework, stood on a platform in the center of the building. An open space, bounded on the outside by a circular wooden fence, surrounded the secondary. Tesla wound the wire for the coil's primary around the fence.

More amazing still was the metal mast that rose from the center of the secondary coil, extending 202 feet (61.6 m) into the air through the laboratory's retractable roof. The bottom of the mast went down through the floor and was embedded in the ground below. A wooden tower surrounded the mast's first 80 feet (24.3 m), and the pole was topped by a three-foot (0.9 m)-wide, hollow wooden ball, coated with copper.

Coils, mast, and ball together made up what Tesla called his "magnifying transformer" or "magnifying transmitter." The mast was the transmitter's antenna. Tesla could adjust its height, as well as various features of the coils, to produce electromagnetic energy with different frequencies. The ball at the mast's top provided a large, curved surface area, ideal for accumulating the tremendous electric charge that the inventor planned to generate in the secondary. (Modern builders of large Tesla coils sometimes use a doughnut-shaped top, which works even better than a sphere.) In essence, the ball acted as a second capacitor. Tesla believed he could use his transformer/transmitter to create electric currents of either large volume (many thousands of amperes) and moderate pressure or moderate volume and tremendous pressure (up to 100 million volts). He hoped it would also amplify electromagnetic signals so they could be transmitted over long distances.

STANDING WAVES

Tesla's laboratory was ready to go into operation by July. He took full advantage of the fierce summer rainstorms that frequently struck the Colorado mountains to study natural lightning. On July 3, one of these storms led him to a discovery that excited him considerably. Recording the storm's electrical activity as it passed his laboratory, he observed that the activity slowly fell as the storm moved away from him but then started rising again, only to fall once more. This pattern repeated many times at regular intervals. He believed that this rising and falling represented stationary or standing waves, much like those he had created for years with his Tesla coils and mechanical oscillators. The waves moved with the storm, showing peaks and troughs of energy as they passed his measuring device. This observation confirmed his opinion that Earth could conduct electricity. It also showed him, as he wrote in his autobiography, that "the Earth is responsive to electrical vibrations of definite pitch just as a tuning fork [is] to certain waves of sound."

Tesla's discovery of standing waves in the Earth convinced him that the planet could act as an electrical resonating unit—essentially, like a gigantic Tesla coil. He used his oscillators to try to learn the planet's resonant frequency and concluded that it was about eight hertz, a figure that researchers in the 1950s found to be nearly correct. He planned to send high-power, high-frequency oscillations into the ground, pumping electricity in and out at a rapid rate. He expected the Earth to resonate with this stimulus, amplifying the original oscillations into ever-greater surges of energy that receivers anywhere on the planet potentially could access. As a result, Tesla wrote in an article published in the May 5, 1904, *Electrical World and Engineer,*

> Not only [would it be] practicable to send telegraphic messages to any distance without wires, as I recognized long ago, but also to impress upon the entire globe the faint modulations of the human voice, far more still, to transmit power, in unlimited amounts to any terrestrial distance and almost without loss.

Tesla claimed that his finding was "of overwhelming importance for the advancement of humanity."

Tesla also thought that the Earth and the atmosphere might be made to work together in transmitting power. He suspected that the upper atmosphere and the ground both would conduct electricity well, whereas the lower atmosphere would not. A capacitor, or condenser, consists of exactly such a "sandwich" of conducting layers separated by an insulating layer. If Tesla's guess was correct, the Earth and atmosphere together might act as a giant capacitor to accumulate and transmit electromagnetic energy.

BLACKOUT

Knowing nothing of the wonderful future that Tesla hoped to create with his experiments, the citizens of Colorado Springs were more worried than thrilled by what they could observe of the mysterious inventor's doings. Flashes of light and rumbles of thunder from his laboratory frequently outdid their natural counterparts in the sky. His magnifying transmitter electrified the Earth for miles around, frightening nearby horses.

Nothing, however, could have prepared the townsfolk for the effects of an experiment that Tesla and an assistant, Kolman Czito, conducted in late summer. Tesla wanted to find out just how much voltage his giant coil could generate by amplifying current through the Earth. He thought it might produce as much as 100 million volts, far more than anyone had made before.

After having Czito turn the coil on briefly to test it, Tesla told his assistant to activate the switch controlling the device's power and leave it on until ordered to turn it off. Margaret Cheney, in her biography *Tesla: Man out of Time,* tells what happened next:

"Now! Close the switch!"

Czito followed orders. . . . The vibration of heavy current surging through the primary coil made the ground feel alive. There came a snap and a roar of lightning exploding above the station. A strange blue light filled the interior of the barnlike structure.

Czito looked up to see the coils a mass of surging, writhing snakes of flame. Electrical sparks filled the air and the sharp smell of ozone stung his nostrils. Lightning exploded again and again, building to a crescendo, and still Czito waited for the order to yank open the switch.

It did not come. Czito feared that Tesla, now watching outside, might have been injured or killed by his artificial lightning. In fact, however, Cheney reports, Tesla was simply paralyzed with awe. He saw lightning bolts shoot out as much as 135 feet (41 m) from the ball, making thunder that he later learned could be heard at least 15 miles (24 km) away.

This tremendous display lasted only a minute. Then, suddenly, both coil and laboratory went completely dark. "Why did you do that?" Tesla shouted to Czito. "I did not tell you to open the switch. Close it again quickly!"

Hobbyists still enjoy building giant Tesla coils, like the one Tesla set up in Colorado Springs, because they produce such exciting displays. This one was demonstrated at the Coachella Music and Arts Festival in Indio, California, on April 18, 2009. (*Jeff Kravitz/FilmMagic/Getty Images*)

Czito replied that he had not touched the switch. A quick telephone call to the Colorado Springs Electric Company solved the mystery: Tesla's equipment had sucked up so much power that it had overloaded the generator for the entire city of Colorado Springs—and set it on fire to boot. Every house in town was as dark as Tesla's laboratory.

The city engineer told the inventor that the town had a backup generator, but he refused to connect it to the laboratory. Tesla could have power again, the engineer said, when the inventor repaired the generator that he had damaged. Tesla did so a few days later. By then, the city leaders may have been regretting the warm welcome they had given the renegade inventor—and they were surely regretting Curtis's promise to let him have all the electricity he wanted for free. Electric company officials told Tesla that thereafter he would receive current from a generator separate from the one that supplied power to the town.

MESSAGE FROM SPACE

Unlike the infamous high-voltage test, the event during Tesla's stay at Colorado Springs that was perhaps most exciting to the inventor himself was not obvious to outsiders. Sometime during late 1899, his sensitive radio receiver picked up a series of faint pulses that seemed too rhythmic to be natural. Tesla was sure that he was hearing a communication from intelligent beings on another planet, probably Mars or Venus. "The feeling is constantly growing on me that I have been the first to hear the greeting of one planet to another," he wrote in an article describing the experience that appeared in *Colliers* magazine on February 19, 1901.

Tesla's biographers have had different theories about what he actually detected. Marc Seifer thinks that, ironically, Tesla's rival, Guglielmo Marconi, or perhaps some other radio pioneer might have broadcast the signals as part of a test, having no idea that Tesla would receive them. Margaret Cheney, on the other hand, believes that Tesla may have been correct in saying that the signals did not originate on Earth—but she thinks they were radio waves emitted naturally by stars or other objects in space, not broadcasts from intelligent beings. Such radio waves later became the basis for the scientific field of radio astronomy.

Even though Tesla kept detailed notes of his work in Colorado Springs, those notes were often incomplete or unclear to outsiders. Tesla scholars therefore remain uncertain about exactly what he attempted and accomplished during those busy months—but his achievements seem to have been

Tesla did many amazing things in Colorado Springs, but he later admitted that this startling photograph was a double exposure: He was not really present in his laboratory when his artificial lightning filled it. *(© Mary Evans Picture Library/Alamy)*

considerable. In addition to learning about the resonance and conductive qualities of the Earth and producing currents that set new records for amperage and voltage, he sent 13 horsepower (about 10,000 watts) of current, enough to light 200 Edison-type incandescent lamps, wirelessly through the Earth for 26 miles (42 km). He also claimed that he had transmitted radio signals up to 600 miles (966 km).

Exciting as these advances were, Tesla made no effort to publicize them at the time or to make other demonstrations that would have convinced the general public—and, more important, potential investors—that his plans for wireless transmission were practical. Indeed, he turned down one important opportunity to do so. During his time in Colorado Springs, he was in communication with the U.S. Navy and Light House Board, which asked him to install a system of wireless telegraphy on one of their ships. Tesla refused, however, even when Commander T. Perry, speaking for the board, said he would rather give the contract to Tesla than to Guglielmo Marconi because Tesla was a U.S. citizen—"home talent," as Perry put it. This reaction, whose motive is unclear, cost Tesla what Marc Seifer calls "the opportunity of a lifetime." The less shy Marconi, meanwhile, captured

MARTIAN FEVER

Long before Nikola Tesla received his eerie signals in Colorado Springs, he felt sure that there were intelligent beings on Mars and perhaps other planets. He stated in the March 29, 1899, *Electrical Review* that he regarded the existence of such beings as a "statistical certainty." In this and other magazine articles dating from as early as 1896, he claimed that one use for his global wireless communication system would be communication with civilizations on other planets.

Tesla was by no means alone in his beliefs. Even some other eminent scientists shared them. During a visit to the United States in September 1897, for instance, no less a personage than Sir William Thomson, Lord Kelvin, perhaps the most famous physicist of his era, offered newspaper reporters several ideas for communicating with civilizations on Mars.

The red planet, in fact, had been the subject of considerable controversy since at least 1877, when its orbit brought it exceptionally close to Earth and a number of astronomers took the opportunity to observe it closely. One of these was Giovanni Schiaparelli (1835–1910), director of the Royal Observatory in Milan, Italy. Schiaparelli saw dark lines on the planet's surface that he thought might be streams of water or other natural geographical features. *Canali*, the word he used to describe these lines, means "channels" in Italian. When English-speaking newspaper reporters wrote stories about Schiaparelli's discovery, however, some of them translated that term as *canals*, which suggests artificial structures.

United States mathematician and astronomer Percival Lowell (1865–1916) studied Mars for 15 years from the observatory he established in Flagstaff, Arizona, beginning in 1894. Unlike Schiaparelli, Lowell stated very plainly his belief that the markings he saw on the planet represented canals and other signs of intelligent life. Lowell published *Mars*, the first of three books describing his theories, in 1895, four years before Tesla's experience in Colorado Springs.

Most astronomers doubted Lowell's claims, but the public did not share their skepticism. Fiction writers of the period built on the common belief that intelligent life existed on Mars, sometimes to terrifying effect. Perhaps the most famous of these was British writer H. G. Wells (1866–1946), whose novel *War of the Worlds* painted a grim picture of Martians invading Earth. Wells's story appeared in book form in 1898, not long before Tesla heard his mystery signals in Colorado Springs.

the attention of the media in August by broadcasting the results of the America's Cup yacht races.

A NEW SUPPORTER

Tesla returned to New York in mid-January 1900. He eagerly told reporters about his messages from outer space and his plans for building a world wireless transmission center that would offer (according to Margaret Cheney) "interconnected radio-telephone networks, synchronized time signals, stock-market bulletins, pocket receivers, private communications, [and] radio news service." At the time, the description of such a communication network must have seemed just as fantastic as Tesla's Martian claims.

The inventor realized, however, that he now needed to "come back to Earth," so he turned once again to the difficult task of trying to raise money to develop his inventions. He attempted to interest the navy in remote-controlled torpedoes, and he thought that the Light House Board might support plans for wireless telegraphy across the Pacific Ocean. Both agencies, however, met his ideas with bureaucratic indifference. George Westinghouse gave him a little money, but not nearly as much as he had hoped for. John Jacob Astor, perhaps irritated because Tesla had spent the previous year generating lightning bolts in Colorado rather than fulfilling his promise to commercialize oscillators and fluorescent lights, avoided him. Nonetheless, Tesla did obtain enough funding to continue his work and apply for three more patents related to wireless communication in early 1900.

Tesla was still famous, and Robert Underwood Johnson asked him to prepare another article for *Century* about his laboratory and research in Colorado Springs. To Johnson's dismay, the essay Tesla wrote, titled "The Problem of Increasing Human Energy," not only was extremely long but was more philosophical than scientific, focusing on his predictions about the technology and energy sources of the future. Somewhat reluctantly, Johnson published it in the magazine's June 1900 issue.

Overlengthy though Tesla's writing may have been, it succeeded in interesting many readers—most notably the financier J. Pierpont Morgan, Thomas Edison's early backer. Morgan told Tesla that he might sponsor the inventor's plans for worldwide message transmission. He emphasized, however, that his goals were more modest than Tesla's utopian visions. He wrote to Tesla at one point that he merely wanted "a way to signal incoming steamers during times of fog, to send messages to Europe, maybe get Wall Street prices when I'm in England."

After several meetings, Morgan agreed in December 1900 to loan Tesla $150,000 in exchange for a 51 percent interest in the inventor's patents related to wireless communication. He told Tesla, however, that he wanted to remain a silent partner; Tesla was not to mention his support to others. He also warned the inventor, "If we proceed, whatever figure we decide upon shall be firm. I will not be bilked for continuing research funds." The two men signed a formal contract to this effect on March 1, 1901.

WARDENCLYFFE

With the first installment of Morgan's money in hand, Tesla began what he hoped would be the greatest project of his life: a giant tower for transmitting messages around the world. In the same month he signed Morgan's contract, he purchased 200 acres of land at Shoreham, Long Island, from James D. Warden, head of the Suffolk County Land Company. The land was about 60 miles (96.6 km) from New York City. Tesla planned for the parcel eventually to house not only the transmission tower and a laboratory but an entire small

Tesla thought of—and patented—the basic concepts of radio transmission before Guglielmo Marconi did, but Marconi, shown here in 1901, was much more successful at publicizing and commercializing his achievements. (*AP Images*)

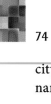

city, providing homes for thousands of workers. To honor Warden, Tesla named his facility Wardenclyffe.

Bad luck and other factors chipped away at Tesla's hopes for Wardenclyffe almost from the beginning. In May, a mere two months after he began the project, a collapse of the stock market brought on a new financial panic. Tesla found his costs rising and his access to the rest of Morgan's money delayed as a result. "Mr. Morgan, you have raised great waves in the industrial world and some have struck my little boat," Tesla wrote to the financier.

"We've all suffered, Mr. Tesla," Morgan replied.

The two men had an argument around July, after Tesla told Morgan that he planned to build a much larger tower than he had proposed earlier. Morgan refused to give him any money beyond the $150,000 the two had already agreed upon—and he was in no hurry to part with the rest of that payment. In truth, he was rapidly becoming disillusioned with the volatile inventor.

While Tesla was dreaming his grand dreams, Guglielmo Marconi was proceeding to make his less extensive form of wireless communication commercially practical. He had sent wireless signals across the English Channel in 1899, and on December 12, 1901, he made worldwide headlines by sending the letter S in Morse code (three "dots," or short signals) wirelessly across the Atlantic Ocean from Poldhu, Cornwall (Britain), to Signal Hill, Newfoundland (Canada).

At first, Tesla was undismayed by Marconi's achievement—or so he said. When H. Otis Pond, an engineer who was helping Tesla at Wardenclyffe, commented that it "looks like Marconi got the jump on you" with the transatlantic transmission, Tesla replied cheerfully, "Marconi is a good fellow. Let him continue. He is using seventeen of my patents."

Marconi in fact admitted in a March 1901 article in *Electrical Review* that he used Tesla coils in his work, although he claimed that such use was "not new" and had been suggested by others besides Tesla. The U.S. Patent Office rejected the Italian's first patent applications because they overlapped Tesla's patents too closely, and Marconi never purchased a license to use Tesla's patented inventions. Pirated technology or no, however, the Marconi Wireless Telegraph Company prospered in the stock markets.

Tesla traveled frequently from his laboratory in New York City to Long Island to check on Wardenclyffe's progress in 1901 and early 1902, often bringing along a picnic lunch and a servant to lay it out. He transferred his headquarters to the laboratory at Wardenclyffe in June 1902.

By September, workers had completed a laboratory building, a powerhouse, and an 187-foot (57-m) wooden tower at Wardenclyffe. The tower,

Tesla intended this tower on Wardenclyffe, Long Island, to be the hub of a worldwide communication empire, but financial difficulties kept him from completing it. *(Kenneth M. Swezey Papers, Archives Center, National Museum of American History, Smithsonian Institution)*

built along the general lines of the earlier one in Colorado Springs, contained a steel shaft that sank 120 feet (36.5 m) into the ground and 16 iron pipes that went down another 300 feet (91.4 m) below the shaft to "grip the earth." The frame of the 100-foot (30.5-m) dome that would cap the tower was raised to its top in early 1903. Tesla intended to cover the frame with copper plates to form an insulated ball, but this stage of construction never took place.

YEARS OF FRUSTRATION

Turning dreams into reality can be a very expensive process, and without Morgan's continued support, Tesla's funds were quickly exhausted. Creditors hounded him constantly, and lack of payments to workers and suppliers increasingly held up progress at Wardenclyffe. In addition to repeatedly attempting to change Morgan's mind, Tesla sought help from other investors. He also tried to earn funds by selling some of his earlier inventions, such as his oscillators. For the most part, however, these efforts were unsuccessful. In July 1903, just after Tesla sent power through his tower and dome for the first and only time, he had to shut down Wardenclyffe and let all his workers go except for a caretaker and George Scherff, Tesla's faithful secretary.

Tesla's constant appeals to Morgan simply seemed to make the financier more determined to resist him. Marc Seifer thinks that at least part of the conflict between the two men arose because Tesla apparently lacked the ability, or perhaps the desire, to understand other people's feelings and motivations. He repeatedly stressed to Morgan that he planned to transmit not only messages but electricity, essentially without cost to the receivers. He failed to consider that free power was the last thing that Morgan, as the owner of most of the country's electric companies, would want. Similarly, Tesla wrote to Morgan in 1904 that he could not develop his radio plans "slowly in grocery-shop fashion" because of Marconi's competition and continued, "I could not report yacht races or signal incoming steamers. There was no money in this. This was no business for a man of your position and importance." Seifer points out, "Morgan loved sailing and yacht races and would resent another [person] suggesting what a man in his position should or should not do."

Tesla stepped up his efforts to obtain funding during the next several years. In late 1903, for instance, he published an elaborate brochure, listing his patents and past accomplishments as well as describing his plans for wireless communication and power transmission and advertising his services as a consulting engineer. Marc Seifer calls this the "Tesla Manifesto." Tesla showed it to, among others, John Jacob Astor and another rich financier, Thomas Fortune Ryan (1851–1928). Ryan said at first that he might consider investing in Tesla's proposals, but he soon changed his mind. Seifer believes that Morgan, who had a powerful influence over Ryan and other money men, quietly discouraged them from giving money to Tesla. Jill Jonnes points out, however, that with the notable exception of his AC system, Tesla had a "terrible track record" in commercializing his inventions. This alone might have made investors think twice about supporting him.

Tesla suffered another major setback in 1904. The U.S. Patent Office, which had previously supported his wireless patents over Marconi's, reversed its previous decisions and granted Marconi a patent for the invention of radio. The reason for this change of heart has never been clear, but several biographers suspect that it may have been related to the fact that a number of influential people, including J. Pierpont Morgan and Thomas Edison, had substantial investments in Marconi's company.

Whether because of Morgan's influence, personal difficulties in interacting with other people, ongoing financial hard times in the country as a whole, or a combination of all these factors, Tesla's efforts to raise money continued to fail. He finally had to close Wardenclyffe completely in 1905. By 1906, he was becoming increasingly depressed, bitter, and mentally unstable. He sent repeated essays and letters to electrical journals and newspapers defending his contributions as an inventor, which were already being forgotten, and containing passionate outcries against the "blind, fainthearted world" that rejected his ideas. His old obsessions and unusual habits grew more intense and new ones were added, including a fondness for feeding the city's population of pigeons.

BLADELESS TURBINE

Tesla was not yet ready to give up. In 1906, he created the first working model of a new invention that he was sure would provide the commercial success he needed to finance the greater dream of Wardenclyffe: a bladeless turbine. John O'Neill and Margaret Cheney believe that the inspiration for this device may have gone all the way back to the bladeless water wheel that Tesla had made as a child. He first described his turbine publicly in a lecture to the National Electric Light Association in May 1911 and patented it in 1913.

Tesla's turbine was a sealed chamber containing a stack of thin metal disks mounted crosswise, like a stack of coins, on a tapered rod. The discs had to be very close together. Nozzles pushed a *fluid* (that is, a liquid, such as water, or a gas, such as steam) under pressure into the turbine from the side.

Tesla's Bladeless Turbine

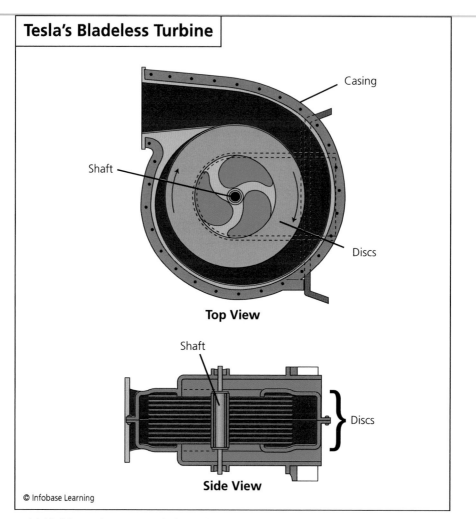

Top View

Side View

© Infobase Learning

Tesla's bladeless turbine consisted of a stack of metal discs mounted on a rod or shaft that ran through their centers. The discs were enclosed in a casing whose walls were very close to their outer rims. This picture shows side and top views of a Tesla turbine that is acting as a pump. A fluid enters the device near its center and follows the path shown in blue. As the fluid moves in a spiral through the stack of discs, it clings to the discs and pulls them around with it, turning the shaft as well. Discs and shaft can turn very rapidly, rotating thousands of times per minute. The fluid then exits through the outer part of the device, following the path shown in red. If the turbine is being used as a motor rather than a pump, the paths are reversed, with the fluid entering near the rim of the turbine and exiting at the center.

Two characteristics of fluids made the liquid or gas pull on the disks. One was *adhesion,* or the tendency of two different surfaces to stick together; adhesion is particularly strong for gases interacting with metal surfaces. The other feature that turned the discs was *viscosity,* the resistance of a fluid to flow; honey, for instance, is more viscous, or thicker, than water. The fluid moved through the stack of discs in a spiral path, tugging the disks—and therefore the rod—around with it as it went, and finally exited at the center of the device. If the rod was attached to a motor, the combination of turbine and motor acted as an engine. If the fluid was introduced at the center of the device instead, its flow was reversed, and the turbine became a pump. Bladed turbines cannot be reversed in this way.

Tesla believed that his new turbine would be "the perfect rotary engine." Because it could be very small and yet produce considerable energy, he once called it his "powerhouse in a hat." His first model, just six inches (15 cm) across and weighing less than 10 pounds (4.5 kg), produced 30 horsepower, more for its size than any other engine known at the time.

Tesla hoped that his turbine would replace standard, bladed steam turbines for driving electrical generators and other purposes. Unfortunately for him, as John O'Neill points out, other inventors had recently designed considerably improved models of these turbines. The new turbines were already in commercial production and had become well entrenched in industry. In order to succeed with his turbine, Tesla would have to persuade the companies that used the other turbines, such as General Electric and Westinghouse, to abandon not only their existing turbine designs but all the manufacturing technology that was built around them—a difficult task at best.

Tesla was elected a member of the New York Academy of Sciences in May 1907, but this did little to improve his mood. In fall 1909, Guglielmo Marconi and a German physicist Carl Ferdinand Braun (1850–1918) won the far more prestigious Nobel Prize in physics for their independent invention of the "wireless telegraph." No one seemed to know or remember that they had built their work on inventions created and patented by Nikola Tesla.

Death Ray

For Nikola Tesla, the second decade of the 20th century offered little change from the first. Tesla struggled to repay or avoid creditors and to obtain funding from rich investors, yet his belief that one or another of his inventions would soon become wildly successful and return him to his former glory remained unshaken. So sure of this was he that he refused to compromise any of his ideas, even when doing so might have brought him the money he needed.

FAILURES AND SUCCESSES

In 1911, Tesla had a chance to win support from mining magnate John Hays Hammond (1865–1936) and his son, John Hays ("Jack") Hammond, Jr. (1888–1965). The elder Hammond gave the inventor some small donations to help him develop his bladeless turbine, and Hammond, Jr., who eventually proved to be as prolific an inventor as Tesla himself, proposed to form a company with Tesla to perfect submersible torpedoes, selective frequency tuning, and other devices. Tesla said that J. Pierpont Morgan and John Jacob Astor had the rights to his wireless patents, but he offered to work with Hammond on remote control and tried to interest the young man in the turbines as well.

Nonetheless, the proposed company never came into existence. Marc Seifer thinks that Tesla would have been well advised to turn to Hammond in his efforts to develop wireless communication, even if it might have meant

Tesla was even less successful in obtaining financing from J. P. Morgan, Jr., shown here in 1938, than he had been with Morgan's father. The elder Morgan loaned Tesla $150,000 to build his Wardenclyffe tower, but the younger Morgan gave the penniless but persistent inventor only small loans. *(AP Images)*

buying out Morgan's 51 percent interest, since Morgan had made it clear that he no longer planned to support Tesla. Either because Tesla was too focused on his own ideas to consider Hammond's more practical ones or simply because he found it almost impossible to work as a partner with anyone, he

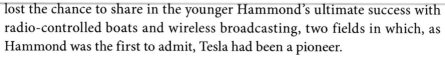

lost the chance to share in the younger Hammond's ultimate success with radio-controlled boats and wireless broadcasting, two fields in which, as Hammond was the first to admit, Tesla had been a pioneer.

Tesla had little better luck with Morgan's own offspring. On June 6, 1913, a little more than a month after the elder Morgan's death, Tesla visited his son and heir, J. P. Morgan, Jr. ("Jack," 1867–1943), in the hope of persuading the younger Morgan to provide the support that his father had so persistently denied. The inventor offered to form two companies with Morgan to develop his bladeless turbines and promised to give Morgan the "entire interest" in both companies. Morgan protested politely that such an arrangement would not be fair to Tesla. Rather, he said, Tesla should form the companies himself—and use the profits, if any, to repay to the Morgan estate the $150,000 that J. Pierpont Morgan had lent him. (Morgan, Jr., did give Tesla several additional small loans in the following years.)

Tesla did have some successes in this period. He sold several licenses for his turbine in Europe, for example. He also started the Tesla Ozone Company in 1910 and the Tesla Propulsion Company a little later. Most important, Telefunken, a large German company that was second only to Marconi's as a leader in wireless communication, began paying him royalties for a license on his radio patents in 1913. Telefunken built several powerful radio transmission towers in the United States, including one in Sayville, New York, just a few miles away from Tesla's beloved Wardenclyffe. The company consulted with Tesla while building the Sayville tower.

Unfortunately for Tesla, changes in world politics soon ended this potentially profitable venture. World War I began in Europe in late July 1914, shortly after the heir to the throne of the Austro-Hungarian Empire was assassinated. Austria-Hungary invaded Serbia (then an independent country) in retaliation, and Germany, an ally of Austria-Hungary, simultaneously invaded Belgium and several other small countries. A number of other major European nations, including Great Britain, in turn declared war on Germany.

The United States remained neutral during the first few years of the war, so Tesla's dealings with Telefunken remained legal. Most U.S. citizens, however, favored Britain and its allies over Germany and regarded all things German with suspicion. The U.S. government seized the Sayville transmitter after breaking off diplomatic relations with Germany in February 1917, suspecting that the Germans were using it for spying. Shortly afterward, on April 6, 1917, the United States declared war on Germany, and Telefunken's payments to Tesla came to an end.

DISAPPOINTMENTS

Tesla, meanwhile, was fighting wars of his own. In 1912, he sued Marconi for patent infringement in several European countries. His suit in France was successful, which provided him with a badly needed emotional boost, but it is not clear whether he received any money as a result. He filed suit in the United States as well in August 1915, but his suit stalled when the U.S. government suspended all patent litigation for the duration of the war. The government made some settlements concerning radio patents after the war, but Tesla was not included because most of his patents had expired by then.

The year 1915 proved to be a bitter one for Tesla. In March, after allowing the poverty-stricken inventor to live on credit for years, the manager of the Waldorf-Astoria Hotel, George C. Boldt (1851–1916), finally lost patience with him and demanded payment. Tesla was forced to sign over to Boldt one of the few items of value he still possessed: the deed to the Wardenclyffe property. Rubbing salt in this wound to his self-esteem, *The World,* a popular New York newspaper, broadcast his financial woes to its reading public.

Later that year, a different newspaper played an important, though unintentional, part in a second painful embarrassment. On November 6, 1915, the *New York Times* announced in a front-page story that Tesla and Thomas Edison were to share that year's Nobel Prize in physics. Tesla had not heard from the Swedish academy that awards these prizes, but he nonetheless believed the report. He waited eagerly for the academy's notification, meanwhile forwarding a copy of the article to J. P. Morgan.

Margaret Cheney says that the *Times* obtained its information from the usually reputable news bureau Reuters, but apparently the newspaper should have checked its facts more carefully. In a second article about a week later, the paper admitted that it had been wrong: The real winners of the 1915 physics prize were William Henry Bragg (1862–1942) and his son, William Lawrence Bragg (1890–1971), who had developed a technique that uses X-rays to determine the structure of crystals. In the wake of this sudden about-face, rumors circulated that Tesla had been offered the prize but refused to accept it. He certainly had made statements suggesting that he might have behaved this way if the occasion had arisen, but in fact he had not even been nominated.

THE EDISON MEDAL

Tesla did receive a major award (not nearly as well known as the Nobel Prize) in 1918—and this time he really did try to reject it. Swiss-born electrical engineer Bernard A. Behrend (1875–1932), a longtime supporter of the inventor's, persuaded the American Institute of Electrical Engineers to give Tesla its Edison Medal as a recognition (long overdue, in Behrend's opinion) of Tesla's lifetime of contributions to the field. When Behrend brought Tesla the news that he was to receive the award, however, the inventor turned on him, venting years of anger at having been ignored by the Institute and the world. According to John O'Neill, he said:

> You propose to honor me with a medal which I could pin upon my coat and strut for a vain hour before the members and guests of your Institute. You would bestow an outward semblance of honoring me but you would decorate my body and continue to let starve, for failure to supply recognition, my mind and its creative products which have supplied the foundation upon which the major portion of your Institute exists.

The fact that the medal was named after Edison, Tesla went on, made the matter even worse: "When you would go through the vacuous pantomime of honoring Tesla you would not be honoring Tesla but Edison who has previously shared unearned glory from every previous recipient of the medal."

The patient Behrend finally persuaded Tesla to accept the award, but his difficulties with the eccentric inventor were by no means over. When the institute presented the medal on May 18, the group first held a banquet at the Engineers' Club, then went across an alley to an auditorium in the United Engineering Societies Building for speeches. As the assembled dignitaries sat down for the second time, Behrend realized with a shock that the guest of honor had vanished.

Behrend and others searched the building and then ventured outside. They eventually found Tesla, dressed in his best suit, engaging in what had become his favorite nighttime activity: feeding the pigeons in Bryant Park, just across the street. Only with difficulty did they persuade him to return and receive the award.

Behrend used his presentation speech to remind his hearers how much they—and the world—owed to Nikola Tesla, who had made his groundbreaking speech about the polyphase alternating-current system to that same body exactly 29 years before. According to John O'Neill, Behrend said in part:

> Were we to seize and eliminate from our industrial world the results of Mr. Tesla's work, the wheels of industry would cease to turn, our electric cars

and trains would stop, our towns would be dark, our mills would be dead and idle. Yes, so far reaching is his work that it has become the warp and woof of industry.

"From [Tesla's] work," Behrend concluded, "has sprung a revolution in the electrical art."

END OF A DREAM

In Tesla's mind, no award could make up for the loss that he suffered in 1917. As a 1921 court case (which Tesla lost) made clear, he believed that he had signed over Wardenclyffe to George Boldt of the Waldorf-Astoria only as collateral to be held in trust until he could pay the hotel the money he owed. He expected Boldt to take care of the property and protect the valuable equipment still on the site from thieves and vandals. Boldt, however, felt that Tesla had simply deeded the property to him as a partial payment of the inventor's back rent. He, Boldt, therefore owned Wardenclyffe free and clear, and he could do with it as he wished. Tesla learned, to his horror, that what Boldt wanted to do with Wardenclyffe—the tower at least—was tear it down and sell the metal for scrap. (The laboratory building is still standing.) A salvage firm, the Smiley Steel Company, offered to do the work.

Desperate to save his beloved tower, Tesla began talking for the first time about a new use that he believed could be made of the same basic ideas that had given rise to Wardenclyffe. Instead of sending messages or power, he said, the Wardenclyffe tower or others like it could be used to broadcast a beam of energy strong enough to knock invading planes out of the air. He tried to interest the government in this potential defense weapon, but he was unsuccessful. Around the end of August, therefore, a crew from the Smiley company set charges of dynamite around the tower and knocked what newspapers had come to call "Tesla's million-dollar folly" to the ground. The time was just after the United States had entered the European war, and rumors circulated that the government had ordered the Wardenclyffe tower destroyed because it feared that German spies were using it. The truth, however, was more mundane—and sadder.

Tesla was not on hand to see the death of his dream. He had at last made arrangements with several businesses to commercialize some of his inventions, including his turbine and an automobile speedometer that used one of his mechanical oscillators. Beginning in July 1917, shortly after he won the Edison Medal, he traveled for several years to help these companies.

TESLA'S VISION OF THE FUTURE

Especially as he grew older, Nikola Tesla loved to share with newspaper reporters his visions of the future. Many of these views were positive, even idealistic: For instance, Tesla predicted that energy would be easily obtainable and free and machines would perform all the boring and difficult tasks of life. Others were darker and more threatening, such as the inventor's support for eugenics, the belief that only physically and mentally healthy people should be allowed to have children.

Tesla offered one of his most wide-ranging sets of predictions in an article that appeared in the popular magazine *Collier's* on January 30, 1926. Some of his expectations for technology now seem uncannily on target: "The household's daily newspaper will be printed 'wirelessly' in the home during the night," he wrote. People would communicate by means of pocket-sized instruments, and "We shall be able to witness and hear events—the inauguration of a President, the playing of a World Series game, the havoc of an earthquake or the terror of a battle—just as though we were present."

The aging inventor's prophesies about society were less accurate. "The struggle of the human female toward sex equality will end in a new sex order, with the female as superior," he wrote in the article, which was titled, "When Woman Is Boss." Female readers were no doubt pleased at Tesla's praise of women's intellect and his statement that once women became as well educated as men, they would "startle civilization with their progress." Most were probably less enthusiastic, however, about what he believed would be the result of this advance:

> The acquisition of new fields of endeavor by women, their gradual usurpation of leadership, will dull and finally dissipate feminine sensibilities, will choke the maternal instinct, so that marriage and motherhood may become abhorrent and human civilization draw closer and closer to the perfect civilization of the bee.

Even most of those who would have been glad to see women become equal or even dominant were unlikely to share Tesla's eagerness to see an insectlike collective society supported by "desexualized armies of workers whose sole aim and happiness in life is hard work."

The inventor's first stop was Chicago, the site of his long-ago Columbian Exposition triumph, where he worked with Pyle National Co. in attempts to manufacture an improved version of his bladeless turbine. He remained there until November 1918, the month World War I ended. Unfortunately for Tesla's hopes, the Pyle engineers found that the metal discs in the turbine were not strong enough to withstand the stress that the rapid rotation of the device placed on them. The tremendous centrifugal force generated by spinning at up to 35,000 revolutions per minute stretched the discs out of shape and eventually made them crack.

A similar effort with the Allis-Chalmers Company in Milwaukee, Wisconsin, in the early 1920s ran into similar problems. After testing a steam-powered version of the turbine, Hans Dahlstrand, the chief engineer at Allis-Chalmers, issued a highly critical report, stating that Tesla's turbine was not much more efficient than other small turbines on the market and was more costly to manufacture. Tesla, in turn, quit the project before any additional tests could be conducted. When John O'Neill later asked the inventor why he had done so, Tesla said only, "They would not build the turbines as I wished."

Tesla's only success was with the Waltham Watch Company of Boston, Massachusetts, which did market Tesla's speedometer and pay him royalties on it. The speedometer was more accurate than those used in most cars of the time, but it was also more expensive to make, so it was installed only on luxury cars.

Tesla's recent achievements might be limited, but he still had his admirers among journalists. John J. O'Neill, who later became his first biographer (and a Pulitzer Prize winner), was one of them. Another was Hugo Gernsback (1884–1967), who shared Tesla's interest in radio, electricity, and unusual inventions and published popular journals on these subjects as well as the first science fiction magazines. Gernsback featured accounts of Tesla's proposed inventions and visions of the future in his magazine *Electrical Experimenter* beginning around 1916, and he published Tesla's autobiography as a series of articles in the same magazine in 1919. To most other observers, however, Tesla seemed eccentric at best and a real-life "mad scientist" at worst. Stories about his odd habits and increasingly impractical-sounding predictions often appeared in newspapers and magazines during the 1920s and 1930s.

A UNIQUE LOVE

The aging Tesla, still impeccably dressed in his old-fashioned clothing, grew increasingly gaunt as he confined himself to an ever-more-limited diet; in

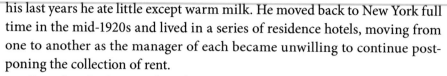

his last years he ate little except warm milk. He moved back to New York full time in the mid-1920s and lived in a series of residence hotels, moving from one to another as the manager of each became unwilling to continue postponing the collection of rent.

Some hotels also were less than happy to have Tesla as a guest because of his habit of feeding and caring for the city's pigeons, which had gone from a hobby to an obsession. Always a night person, the inventor went out around midnight every night to feed the birds near the New York Public Library, Bryant Park, and St. Patrick's Cathedral. "These are my sincere friends," he once told a visitor, according to Margaret Cheney. If a pigeon was injured, he brought it up to his room and took care of it until it could be released. Hotel maids did not appreciate having to clean up the birds' droppings.

Tesla treasured all his pigeons, but one bird, a white female with a little gray on the tips of her wings, was special. Tesla told John O'Neill and another science journalist, William L. Laurence (1888–1977), "No matter where I was, that pigeon would find me; when I wanted her I had only to wish and call her and she would come flying to me. She understood me and I understood her."

Indeed, O'Neill wrote in his biography of Tesla, the elderly man went on to make a startling confession:

> I loved that pigeon . . . as a man loves a woman, and she loved me. When she was ill I knew, and understood. . . . That pigeon was the joy of my life. If she needed me, nothing else mattered. As long as I had her, there was a purpose in my life.

Pigeon lives are short compared to those of humans, however, and in time Tesla lost his beloved. His last sight of her was an overwhelmingly strange experience that he recounted to O'Neill:

> One night as I was lying in my bed in the dark, . . . she flew in through the open window and stood on my desk. I knew . . . she wanted to tell me something important so I got up and went to her.
>
> As I looked at her I knew she wanted to tell me—she was dying. And then, as I got her message, there came a light from her eyes—powerful beams of light. . . .
>
> It was a real light, a powerful, dazzling blinding light, a light more intense than I had ever produced by the most powerful lamps in my laboratory.

Tesla claimed that he loved this female pigeon "as a man loves a woman" and that when she died, "I knew that my life's work was finished." *(MNT, VI/VIII, 101, © Nikola Tesla Museum, Belgrade)*

"When that pigeon died, something went out of my life," Tesla concluded. "Up to that time I knew with a certainty that I would complete my work, no matter how ambitious my program, but . . . [then] I knew my life's work was finished."

FLIVVER PLANES AND DEADLY RAYS

Tesla obtained his last patent in 1928. It was for what would now be called a *VTOL* (vertical takeoff and landing) *aircraft*; Tesla termed it his "flivver plane" or "flying stove." The design in the patent indicates that the craft could act like both a helicopter and a fixed-wing plane. When it took off or landed, its propeller was at the top, like the rotor of a helicopter. In that position, the propeller could lift the craft straight up into the air or set it down on the roof of a building or the deck of a boat. Once the craft was airborne, propelled by one of Tesla's bladeless turbines, the pilot activated a tilting device that turned the plane so that the propeller was in front, yet kept the pilot's seat vertical. Wings like those of an airplane then extended horizontally. As with so many of Tesla's inventions, he never developed this aircraft beyond the idea stage. He once called it "the child of my dreams."

Far more alarming than the flivver plane was Tesla's proposed "tele-force" ray, an expansion of his 1917 defense idea that he first described in 1934. He claimed that this weapon could "bring down a fleet of 10,000 enemy airplanes at a distance of 200 miles . . . and . . . cause armies to drop dead in their tracks." To be sure, he always presented the ray as something that would be used only for defense; indeed, he often said that this invention would end war because no one would be able to attack a nation that possessed it. Before long, however, the press began calling his imagined invention a "death ray."

No model of Tesla's ray was ever discovered, but he wrote a scientific paper about it in 1937. This unpublished paper, titled "The Art of Projecting Concentrated Non-Dispersive Energy through the Natural Media," was found among the inventor's effects after his death. It explained that Tesla's proposed device, which he intended to mount on a Wardenclyffe-style tower, had a unique vacuum chamber with one open end. A special nozzle attached to this opening, sealed around the edges with a high-velocity air stream to preserve the vacuum, would fire streams of particles or tiny droplets (probably of liquid mercury or tungsten) that were charged to millions of volts. Pumping action from a Tesla turbine, combined with a powerful electrostatic repelling force, would give these pellets enough velocity to travel hundreds of miles.

Tesla's slide into obscurity and ridicule halted briefly on his 75th birthday—July 10, 1931—thanks to Kenneth Swezey (1905–72), a young science writer who had become another of the aged inventor's admirers and close friends. Swezey asked famous scientists and other notables to send testimonials for the birthday celebration. He received a flood of responses, of which this one from Swedish-American radio and television engineering pioneer E. F. W. Alexanderson is typical:

> In almost every step of progress in electrical power engineering, as well as in radio, we can trace the spark of thought back to Nikola Tesla. There are few indeed who in their lifetime see realization of such a far-flung imagination.

Swezey mounted the letters in a book and gave it to Tesla; the book was still in a safe in Tesla's room when he died. *Time* magazine also honored Tesla on this birthday by putting his picture on its cover.

Time magazine put Nikola Tesla on the cover of this issue in July 1931 to honor the inventor's 75th birthday. (© Nikola Tesla Museum, Belgrade)

In the late 1930s and early 1940s, Tesla had increasing dealings with political factions in Yugoslavia, which became an independent kingdom after World War I and included his old homeland. This came about partly because one of Tesla's nephews, Sava Kosanović, became the Yugoslavian ambassador to the United States, and the two met and became good friends.

Yugoslavia was eager to honor Tesla, whom its citizens saw as a national hero. The Yugoslavian government established a research laboratory called the Tesla Institute in Belgrade (now the capital of Serbia) in 1936, and on Tesla's 81st birthday, in 1937, the government gave Tesla the country's highest award, the Grand Cordon of the White Eagle. More usefully, it promised to pay him $600 a month for the rest of his life, thus ending his most immediate money worries. (In 1934, the Westinghouse Company had also agreed to pay Tesla a small ongoing monthly salary as a consulting engineer, as well as covering his rent at the Hotel New Yorker.) Nearby Czechoslovakia (now the Czech Republic and Slovakia) awarded the inventor the Grand Cordon of the White Lion at the same time.

As the clouds of World War II (1939–45) began to gather in the late 1930s, Tesla tried to interest several governments in his "death ray." Papers seized after his death suggest that he sold plans for the device to the Amtorg Trading Corporation, a business controlled by the Soviet Union. The Public Broadcasting System Web site for the program *Tesla—Master of Lightning* states that the corporation paid Tesla $25,000 for this information. An article in the May 2, 1977, *Aviation Week* claimed that at that time the Soviet Union was experimenting with a *particle-beam weapon* (a weapon that uses a high-energy beam of atoms or electrons) that bore a "remarkable resemblance" to Tesla's then-unpublished drawings. The United States also experimented with particle-beam weapons as part of the Strategic Defense Initiative (the so-called Star Wars defense system) in the 1980s.

RADAR

Tesla's death ray played no part in World War II or any other war, but another of his ideas did. In August 1917, while the previous world war was still raging, Tesla had written in Hugo Gernsback's *Electrical Experimenter:*

> If we can shoot out a concentrated ray comprising a stream of minute electric charges vibrating electrically at tremendous frequency, say millions of cycles per second, and then intercept this ray, after it has been reflected by a submarine hull for example, and cause this intercepted ray to illuminate

Radio Detection and Ranging (RADAR)

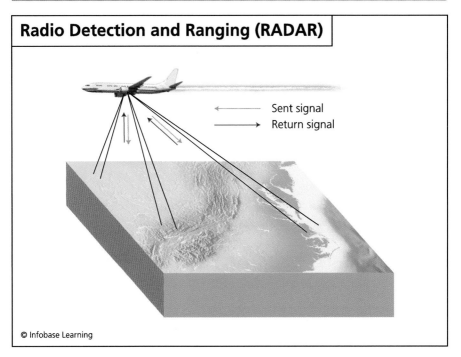

Sent signal
Return signal

© Infobase Learning

Several inventors developed radar (**RA**dio **D**etection **A**nd **R**anging) in 1934, building on a concept that Nikola Tesla had described in 1917. Radar, which involves bouncing radio waves off distant objects and analyzing the echoes that return, was first used in World War II to detect enemy ships and planes, but today it is often employed to analyze land formations, as shown here.

a fluorescent screen (similar to the X-ray method) on the same or another ship, then our problem of locating the hidden submarine will have been solved.

This was the underlying concept of what came to be known as *radar* (radio detection and ranging).

Tesla never developed his idea further, but others did. In 1934, the year in which the eccentric inventor first proposed his death ray, French, Soviet, and U.S. engineers independently developed a system for detecting distant ships, planes, or other objects containing metal that was similar to what Tesla had described. It sent radio waves into the air and used an antenna to detect echoes from waves that reflected off objects. One of these inventors, Émile Girardeau (1882–1970), wrote that his device was "conceived according to the principles stated by Tesla." Others improved this invention, and it played a valuable role in defense during World War II. Tesla was mistaken in

Soldiers in World War II depended on several inventions that can be traced to Nikola Tesla, including radar and radio sets like the one these men are using on an Italian hillside in 1944. While this war was raging, Tesla died alone and almost forgotten in his New York hotel room. *(Library of Congress)*

thinking that radio waves would work in this way under water, but *sonar,* a similar technology that uses sound waves instead of radio waves, can detect submarines.

DEATH OF A LONELY MAN

The elderly inventor became increasingly isolated as more and more of his friends passed away. Katharine Johnson had died in 1925, for instance, and Robert Underwood Johnson followed in 1937. Although Sava Kosanović, Kenneth Swezey, and John O'Neill visited as often as they could, it sometimes seemed that Tesla really trusted only his pigeons. He had health problems as well, especially after a taxicab hit him during one of his midnight excursions in late 1937, wrenching his back and breaking three ribs. He refused to see a doctor and remained bedridden for six months. He paid young telegram deliverers from Western Union to take over his daily pigeon feedings when he could not visit the birds himself.

In early January 1943, Tesla startled one of these helpers by summoning him to his hotel room one evening. He gave the young man an envelope and told him to deliver it immediately to his friend Samuel Clemens—Mark Twain—at a certain address. Attempting to carry out the inventor's wish, the messenger learned that the street Tesla had mentioned no longer existed, at least under that name; the address actually was that of Tesla's first laboratory. Clemens, furthermore, had been dead since 1910.

When the youth returned to Tesla and tried to explain these things, the old man would not listen. Clemens "was in my room here, last night," he insisted, according to John O'Neill's biography. "He sat in that chair and talked to me for an hour. He is having financial difficulties and needs my help. So you go right back to that address and deliver that envelope—and don't come back until you have done so." The puzzled messenger took the letter to the hotel manager's office, where he and the manager opened the envelope. It contained a blank sheet of paper wrapped around 20 $5 bills—a generous donation from the financially strapped Tesla to his old friend.

A day or two later, Tesla told the maid who had come to clean his room to place a "Do Not Disturb" sign on his door and tell the hotel staff not to enter unless he called for them. On January 8, however, one maid became concerned and went into the room anyway. She found Tesla dead in his bed. The medical examiner concluded that the 86-year-old inventor had died the night before from a heart attack.

GOVERNMENT MYSTERIES

Tesla's death brought a parade of visitors to his room—and spawned mysteries and conspiracy theories that linger to this day. Kenneth Swezey took the book of 75th-birthday testimonials from a safe in the hotel room, which also contained Tesla's precious citizenship papers. Sava Kosanović collected several photographs. A team of government officials, including some from the Federal Bureau of Investigation (FBI), seized virtually everything else that Tesla had left, including all his papers and working models of several of his inventions. According to Margaret Cheney, two young American engineers engaged in war work who, with the old man's permission, had been examining his papers a few weeks before his death had alerted the FBI. They told the agency they were concerned that "critical scientific information might fall into foreign hands," Cheney writes.

Tesla's funeral, sponsored by the Yugoslav government, was held on January 12 at the Cathedral of Saint John the Divine. More than 2,000 people attended, including officials from both General Electric and Westinghouse. President Franklin Roosevelt (1882–1945) sent condolences through his wife, Eleanor (1884–1962). In an editorial on Tesla's death, the *New York Sun* wrote:

> Mr. Tesla was eighty-six years old when he died. He died alone. He was an eccentric, whatever that means. . . . Tesla, the ostensibly foolish old gentleman . . . was trying with superb intelligence to find the answers. His guesses were right so often that he would be frightening. Probably we shall appreciate him better a few million years from now.

The inventor's body was cremated. In 1957, more than a decade later, his ashes were sent to the Tesla Museum in Belgrade.

The U.S. government continued to take great interest in Tesla's papers, perhaps fearing, in that time of war, that his death ray might not be a complete delusion after all. The FBI gave Tesla's effects to the Office of Alien Property (OAP), an agency that took over possessions of people suspected of being enemies of the country or allies of such enemies. Tesla's biographers consider this action strange, since Tesla had been a naturalized U.S. citizen for decades and had never been accused of spying. The government may have thought that, possibly through Kosanović, Tesla had leaked dangerous information about his proposed weapon to the Soviet Union, which the United States increasingly distrusted.

Around February, government officials asked John G. Trump, head of the High Voltage Research Laboratory at the Massachusetts Institute of Technology (MIT), to examine Tesla's property. Accompanied by an entourage that included two members of the OAP and three representatives of Naval Intelligence, Trump did so, even daring to open the box stored in a vault at the Hotel Governor Clinton, one of Tesla's residences, that the inventor had claimed to contain a working model of the death ray set to go into action if any unauthorized person unsealed the box. The only object in the box was an old-fashioned and completely harmless piece of electrical equipment—but opinions still differ on whether Tesla placed the equipment there as a joke or whether earlier government visitors had taken away an actual death ray model and replaced it with this device.

In any case, Trump concluded that Tesla's effects contained nothing important to national security. "I can therefore see no technical or military reason why further custody of the property should be retained," he wrote in his report. Trump admitted later that he had examined only a

In 1952, the Federal People's Republic of Yugoslavia established the Tesla Museum, shown here, to honor the inventor. The museum still exists in Belgrade, now the capital of Serbia. *(Kenneth M. Swezey Papers, Archives Center, National Museum of American History, Smithsonian Institution)*

small part of the truckloads of material that had been collected from Tesla's hotels and storage lockers, but the items he reviewed did include the 1937 paper in which Tesla had spelled out the design of his death ray fairly precisely.

After a court hearing, the government returned Tesla's effects to Kosanović, whom they considered to be the inventor's heir (Tesla had left no will). In 1952, Kosanović contributed them to the Tesla Museum, which the government of what was by then the Federal People's Republic of Yugoslavia established in that year to preserve the inventor's heritage.

Tesla biographers say that the FBI or other agencies photocopied some of Tesla's papers. In October 1945, just after the end of World War II, a representative of the Air Technical Service Command headquarters at Wright Field (Ohio) requested the OAP's copy of the papers to be used "in connection with projects for National Defense." The OAP sent the papers—or said it did—but it is not clear whether the papers ever reached Wright Field or what finally became of them.

ENDURING LEGACY

Just a few months after Tesla died, his memory received an important vindication. On June 21, 1943, the U.S. Supreme Court ruled in the case of *Marconi Wireless Telegraph Co. of America v. United States* that Tesla's patents on the basic technology of radio preceded Guglielmo Marconi's. In essence, by striking down Marconi's patent because of Tesla's priority, the court declared that Tesla, not Marconi, was the true father of radio.

Interest in Tesla and his inventions, both real and imagined, has resurfaced periodically. In 1956, celebrations occurred in several parts of the world to honor the 100th year since his birth. The Institute Electrotechnical Committee in Munich, Germany, agreed to call the unit of magnetic flux density, which measures the strength of a magnetic field, a *tesla*. Tesla was inducted posthumously into the National Inventors Hall of Fame in 1975, and in 1976, a statue of him by sculptor Franko Krsinic, a gift from Yugoslavia, was placed at Niagara Falls. A similar statue was set up in Gospić, Tesla's home village, but it was destroyed during the war that swept the area in the 1990s.

Despite his business failures and the ridicule he often experienced in his later life, Nikola Tesla sensed that he would never be forgotten and indeed that his reputation would grow over time. "Let the future tell the truth and evaluate each [inventor] according to his work and accomplishments," he once told a friend. "The present is theirs [his rivals'], the future, for which I really worked, is mine."

Conclusion

One of Nikola Tesla's greatest weaknesses was that he seldom had the patience to guide his inventions through the long process of commercialization. He could not bear to waste time dealing with such matters as refinement of models, manufacturing costs, and advertising when hosts of new ideas swarmed in his mind, begging to be explored. This very failure, however, has combined with the amazingly prodigious output of his fertile brain to produce what may be the Serbian inventor's greatest legacy: an endless well of inspiration for other inventors.

Inventors began drinking from that well during Tesla's lifetime, often to his own loss. Seizing and expanding on Tesla's basic circuit designs, Guglielmo Marconi and others perfected radio. Jack Hammond developed remote-controlled devices far past the level of Tesla's little boat. Succeeding engineers, in turn, extended radio into television and remote control into everything from robot surgical tools to unmanned craft that explore the deep sea and other planets. Some inventors took Tesla's concepts in entirely new directions, as when they embodied ideas shown in his 1892 carbon button lamps in such later creations as the cyclotron and the point electron microscope.

Tesla fascinates engineers and hobbyists of today as much as ever, and some are coming close to fulfilling dreams that Tesla outlined but lacked the patience, the money, or the technology to make real. For instance, a New Hampshire company called Solar Aero has created a wind turbine based on

Tesla's bladeless turbine design. In an article published in May 2010 on the Web site www.physorg.com, Solar Aero claimed that the turbine can generate electricity at a cost comparable to that for coal-generated plants, something wind power has not usually been able to achieve. The turbine is also expected to have lower maintenance costs than standard bladed turbines, and it cannot harm birds or bats as bladed wind turbines sometimes do because the turbine is enclosed.

Perhaps Tesla's greatest unfulfilled dreams were his plans for worldwide wireless transmission of signals and electric power. Inventors have realized his vision of wireless signal networks in the satellites that broadcast radio and television from one part of the world to another, the towers that transmit cell phone messages, and the Internet's instant communication. Commercially practical wireless transmission of electricity, on the other hand, has not yet been achieved.

Researchers are still investigating ways of combining the Earth and the *ionosphere*—the uppermost layer of the atmosphere—to transmit signals, just as Tesla tried to do in Colorado Springs and at Wardenclyffe. The High Frequency Active Auroral Research Program (HAARP), a government-sponsored science program established in 1993, beams high-frequency electromagnetic waves into the ionosphere directly above its research station in Gakona, Alaska, and observes the changes that this disturbance produces, such as an increase in heat. The project's aims are to learn more about natural processes that occur in the ionosphere and to study this atmospheric layer's interaction with radio signals in the hope of improving long-distance communication. Dennis Papadopoulos, a professor of physics at the University of Maryland and senior science adviser to HAARP, told a Public Broadcasting System interviewer that his work draws strongly on Tesla's. "Once we create the waves, they propagate exactly the way Tesla conceived it," he said.

Papadopoulos feels that Tesla's hope of transmitting large amounts of electric power wirelessly over large distances will never be achieved because both the Earth and the ionosphere are poorer conductors than Tesla thought. Most of the energy therefore bleeds away during its travels. However, Marin Soljačić (1974–   ), an assistant professor of physics at the Massachusetts Institute of Technology (MIT), thinks that wireless transmission of a significant amount of energy is practical over short distances, and he and his coworkers are doing their best to make such transmission a commercial reality.

Soljačić, who like Tesla is a Croatian by birth, uses transmitter and receiver coils that are set to resonate at the same frequency, just as Tesla did.

Soljačić, however, concentrates his tuning on the coils' magnetic fields rather than on their electric current, "strongly coupling" the coils so they share what becomes almost a single magnetic field. He and his coworkers have also found a way to increase the efficiency of their energy transfer by focusing the transfer rather than allowing the energy to radiate in all directions, as the electromagnetic waves from Tesla's system did.

In 2007, Soljačić's group demonstrated that they could light a 60-watt bulb with energy transmitted wirelessly from a power source seven feet (2 m) away. They formed a company called WiTricity in that same year to commercialize their invention. They reported in 2010 that they could power a 32-inch (81-cm) television at the same distance. They claim that for many types of use, they can achieve an energy transfer efficiency of more than 90 percent—a standard that even Tesla would have envied. They hope to create wireless rechargers for everything from cell phones to electric cars.

Solar Aero, HAARP, and WiTricity are just a few of the innovative groups using Nikola Tesla's work as a source of intriguing ideas. They or others may develop some of those ideas into technologies that will prove as important in shaping the society of tomorrow as Tesla's AC power system was in spawning the world of the 20th century. The well of inspiration that Tesla created surely will never run dry.

Chronology

600 B.C.E.
Greek philosopher Thales observes that amber attracts objects if rubbed

early 1600s
William Gilbert shows that other kinds of objects can be electrified (made to act like amber)

1752
Benjamin Franklin demonstrates that lightning is a form of electricity

1781
Luigi Galvani shows that animal tissues respond to electricity

1800
Alessandro Volta creates first battery

1807
Humphrey Davy shows that chemical reactions can produce electricity and electric current can break down chemical compounds

1820s
Scientists discover that electric currents generate magnetic fields around themselves

1831
Michael Faraday shows that moving or changing magnetic fields generates electric currents; invents electrical generator (dynamo)

late 1830s
Samuel F. B. Morse perfects the telegraph

July 9–10, 1856
Nikola Tesla born at midnight in Smiljan (now part of Croatia)

1861
Tesla's older brother, Dane, killed in accident

1862
Tesla family moves to Gospić

1864
James Clerk Maxwell discovers properties of electromagnetic spectrum

1870
Tesla recovers from serious illness; begins studies at Higher Real Gymnasium in Karlovac

1873
Tesla returns home, nearly dies of cholera; his father agrees to let him study engineering

1875
Tesla enrolls in Polytechnic Institute in Graz, Austria

1876
After seeing demonstration of Gramme dynamo/motor, Tesla suggests improvement that his professor rejects; develops gambling addiction

1880
Tesla attends University of Prague; his father dies

1881
Tesla works in Budapest as a draftsman and running a telephone exchange; suffers illness that makes his senses extremely acute; Edison begins supplying homes and businesses in New York City with direct-current electric power

February 1882
Tesla recovers from illness; invents alternating-current (AC) induction motor

March–April 1882
Tesla invents polyphase motors and system for generating, transmitting, and using AC electricity

September 4, 1882
Edison opens first electricity generating station on Pearl Street (New York City)

late 1882
Tesla obtains work with Continental Edison Company in Paris

early 1883
Tesla travels to Strasbourg to repair railroad station lighting installation; builds model of AC motor

spring 1884
Tesla returns to Paris; is denied promised reward

June 1884
Tesla goes to New York; meets Edison; Edison hires him; he repairs dynamos on ship

late 1884
Tesla quits job with Edison after being told that promise of a large payment was meant as a joke

March 30, 1885
Tesla applies for first patent on improved arc lamp

spring 1885
Investors form company to produce Tesla's arc lamp

spring 1886
Investors vote Tesla out of arc lamp company

spring 1886–spring 1887
Tesla forced to dig ditches for a living

November 1886
George Westinghouse sets up first AC power station in Buffalo, New York

April 1887
Investors form Tesla Electric Company

November 1887
Edison tells New York State Death Commission that execution by AC electricity would be quick, sure, and painless

late 1887
Tesla's company files patents covering complete system for generating, transmitting, and using AC electricity

early 1888
Tesla's AC patents granted; William Anthony tests Tesla's AC motor

February 1888
Edison issues booklet warning of the dangers of alternating current

May 16, 1888
Tesla gives landmark lecture on AC motors and transformers to American Institute of Electrical Engineers (AIEE)

June 1888
Harold P. Brown tells New York City Board of Electrical Control about risks from alternating current

July 1888
Tesla meets Westinghouse and agrees to sell Westinghouse his patents; Westinghouse replies to criticisms of AC's safety; New York State legislature votes to use electrocution as the state's method of execution for people convicted of capital crimes

July 30, 1888
Harold Brown attempts to demonstrate the dangers of AC by publicly electrocuting a dog

late 1888–late 1889
Tesla stays in Philadelphia to act as consultant for Westinghouse

December 12, 1888
New York Medico-Legal Society committee votes to use AC in state executions

1890
Cataract Construction Company forms to harness Niagara Falls for production of electric power

August 6, 1890
William Kemmler becomes first person to die in electric chair

late 1890
Financial panic begins

1891
Tesla patents Tesla coil

early 1891
Tesla gives up his AC patent royalties to help Westinghouse keep control of his firm

May 20, 1891
In talk to AIEE, Tesla demonstrates ancestors of fluorescent and neon lights

July 15, 1891
Westinghouse blocks attempt to seize control of his company

July 30, 1891
Tesla becomes naturalized U.S. citizen

summer 1891
Westinghouse Corporation installs first commercial Tesla AC generator and motor in Telluride, Colorado

August 1891
C. E. L. Brown and Mikhael von Dolivo-Dobrowolsky, using an AC system based on Tesla's design, transmit 190 horsepower of electricity from Lauffen to Frankfurt (Germany), a distance of 112 miles (180 km)

February 1892
General Electric formed

spring 1892
Tesla gives lectures to the Institute of Electrical Engineers and the Royal Society in London and the International Society of Engineers in Paris

May 22, 1892
Westinghouse wins contract to provide lighting for Chicago's Columbian Exposition

June 1892
Success of Telluride operation announced

summer 1892
Tesla's mother dies

spring 1893
In lecture to National Electric Light Association in St. Louis, Missouri, Tesla demonstrates basic circuits necessary for radio transmission and reception

May 1, 1893
Columbian Exposition opens

May 6, 1893
Cataract Construction Co. decides to use polyphase AC system at Niagara Falls

October 27, 1893
Cataract Construction Co. gives Westinghouse the contract to build power-house for Niagara Falls project

October 31, 1893
World's Columbian Exposition

1894
Westinghouse begins construction of turbines and generators at Niagara; *Inventions, Researches, and Writings of Nikola Tesla* published; Tesla wins Elliott Cresson Gold Medal from Franklin Institute and honorary doctorates from Columbia and Yale; Edward Dean Adams offers Tesla $100,000 for a controlling interest in his newer patents

February 1895
Tesla forms Nikola Tesla Company with Adams and other investors

March 13, 1895
Fire destroys Tesla's laboratory

July 1895
Tesla opens new laboratory

August 26, 1895
Power station at Niagara Falls goes into operation

1896
Tesla transmits radio signals over 25 miles; patents oscillators and other inventions related to radio; studies X-rays

February 1896
Tesla visits Colorado Springs, Colorado, to evaluate it as a possible site for a laboratory

July 1896
Tesla visits Niagara installation

November 16, 1896
Niagara power station begins transmitting electricity to Buffalo

December 1896
Guglielmo Marconi applies for patent on radio transmission and reception

September 1897
Tesla files patents for generating, storing, transmitting, and receiving wire-less signals

May 1898

Tesla demonstrates radio-controlled boat, ancestor of robots and multichannel broadcasting systems, in Madison Square Garden, New York

December 1898

John Jacob Astor offers to fund development of Tesla's oscillators and cold lights but refuses to pay for his research on wireless transmission

1899

Marconi sends wireless signals across English Channel

January 1899

Astor gives Tesla $100,000 for shares of stock in Tesla's company; Tesla moves into Waldorf-Astoria Hotel

early 1899

Tesla is offered laboratory space and free electric power in Colorado Springs and decides to move there

May 18, 1899

Tesla arrives in Colorado Springs

July 3, 1899

Tesla observes standing waves during a storm, proving to his satisfaction that the Earth can conduct electricity and respond to resonance

late summer 1899

Tesla blacks out Colorado Springs town dynamo with a high-voltage test

late 1899

Tesla detects what he thinks are signals from intelligent beings on another planet

1900

Tesla's 1897 radio patents are granted

mid-January 1900

Tesla returns to New York

June 1900

Tesla publishes long article on increasing human energy in *Century* magazine; it attracts interest of J. Pierpont Morgan

December 1900

Morgan agrees to loan Tesla $150,000 in exchange for a 51 percent interest in Tesla's patents on wireless communication

March 1, 1901
Tesla signs formal agreement with Morgan and receives first payment

March 1901
Tesla purchases land on Long Island for worldwide transmission tower and names it Wardenclyffe; Marconi admits in print that his system includes Tesla coils

May 1901
Financial panic delays delivery of the rest of Morgan's money

July 1901
Morgan and Tesla argue after Tesla reveals plans for larger tower; Morgan refuses to increase loan

December 12, 1901
Marconi transmits wireless signals across Atlantic Ocean

June 1902
Tesla moves laboratory headquarters to Wardenclyffe

September 1902
Workers complete laboratory building, powerhouse, and tower at Wardenclyffe

1903
Tesla receives patent for method of tuning radio receivers to respond to combinations of frequencies

early 1903
Dome frame raised to top of tower at Wardenclyffe

July 1903
Tesla sends power through Wardenclyffe tower and dome for first time, then has to close down most of the facility

late 1903
Tesla publishes elaborate brochure stressing his accomplishments in effort to obtain financial support

1904
Reversing previous decision supporting Tesla, U.S. Patent Office grants basic patent for radio to Marconi

1905
Tesla forced to close Wardenclyffe completely

1906
Tesla creates first working model of bladeless turbine

May 1907
Tesla elected a member of New York Academy of Sciences

October 1909
Marconi wins share of Nobel Prize in physics for invention of radio

1910
Tesla starts two new companies

1911
Tesla and John Hays Hammond, Jr., consider forming a joint company, but the company never comes into existence

May 1911
Tesla describes bladeless turbine publicly for the first time

1912
Tesla sues Marconi for patent infringement in several European countries and wins suit in France

1913
Tesla patents bladeless turbine; Telefunken, a German wireless company, begins paying Tesla royalties for use of his radio patents

April 1913
J. Pierpont Morgan dies

June 6, 1913
Tesla attempts unsuccessfully to form partnership with J. P. Morgan, Jr.

July 1914
World War I begins in Europe

March 1915
Tesla signs over deed to Wardenclyffe to George Boldt, manager of Waldorf-Astoria, as part payment of back rent

August 1915
Tesla sues Marconi for patent infringement in United States

November 6, 1915
New York Times announces that Tesla and Edison will share that year's Nobel Prize in physics

mid-November 1915
Times admits that its Nobel Prize story was mistaken

1917
U.S. government suspends patent litigation, including Tesla's suit against Marconi

February 1917
U.S. breaks off diplomatic relations with Germany and seizes Telefunken's Sayville radio transmission tower

April 6, 1917
U.S. declares war on Germany; Tesla's payments from Telefunken end

July 1917
Tesla goes to Chicago to help Pyle National Co. attempt to manufacture his bladeless turbine

August 1917
At George Boldt's order, Smiley Steel Company destroys Wardenclyffe tower for salvage; Tesla describes the basic idea of radar

May 18, 1918
Tesla reluctantly receives Edison Medal from American Institute of Electrical Engineers

November 1918
World War I ends; Tesla returns to New York

1919
Hugo Gernsback publishes Tesla's autobiography serially in *Electrical Experimenter*

1921
Tesla sues George Boldt for not safeguarding the Wardenclyffe property after Tesla gave him the deed to it; judge rules that the property belonged to Boldt and he could do with it whatever he wished

early 1920s
Tesla and Allis-Chalmers Co. attempt to manufacture turbine but encounter engineering problems

mid-1920s
Tesla becomes obsessed with feeding and caring for pigeons

1928
Tesla obtains his last patent, for a "flivver plane" that is an ancestor of VTOL aircraft

July 10, 1931
Kenneth Swezey persuades notable scientists and others to write tributes to Tesla, which Swezey mounts in a book and gives the inventor to honor Tesla's 75th birthday; *Time* magazine puts Tesla on its cover

1934
Tesla describes "teleforce" ray in detail for the first time; Westinghouse Co. agrees to pay Tesla a small ongoing salary as a consultant and cover his hotel rent; radar developed "according to principles suggested by Tesla"

1936
Yugoslavia establishes Tesla Institute in Belgrade

1937
Tesla writes scientific paper describing death ray

July 10, 1937
Yugoslavia gives Tesla the Grand Cordon of the White Eagle and promises to pay him $600 a month for the rest of his life; Czechoslovakia awards him the Grand Cordon of the White Lion

late 1937
A taxicab hits Tesla, wrenching his back and breaking three ribs

January 7, 1943
Tesla dies of a heart attack in his New York hotel room

January 8, 1943
FBI agents and other government officials seize most of Tesla's papers and models

January 12, 1943
Tesla's funeral held at Cathedral of St. John the Divine

February 1943
At government request, electrical expert John Trump examines some of Tesla's effects; he concludes that they contain nothing important to national security

June 21, 1943
U.S. Supreme Court rules that Tesla's radio patents have priority over Marconi's

October 1945
Air Technical Services Command requests copy of Tesla's papers to be used "in connection with projects for National Defense"

1952
Yugoslavia establishes Tesla Museum; Saha Kosanović gives Tesla's effects to the museum

1956
Celebrations honor 100th anniversary of Tesla's birth; his name is given to unit of magnetic flux density (strength of magnetic field)

1957
Tesla Museum receives Tesla's ashes

1975
Tesla inducted into National Inventors Hall of Fame

1976
Statue of Tesla placed at Niagara Falls

late 1970s, 1980s
United States and Soviet Union experiment with particle-beam weapons similar to Tesla's proposed death ray

1993
Government establishes High Frequency Active Auroral Research Program (HAARP) to study effect of electromagnetic radiation on ionosphere, a subject that interested Tesla

2007
Scientists at MIT demonstrate highly efficient wireless transmission of electricity over short distances

2010
Solar Aero develops wind turbine based on Tesla's bladeless turbine design; WiTricity powers 32-inch (81-cm) television wirelessly from a power source seven feet (2 m) away

Glossary

adhesion the tendency of two different surfaces to stick together.

alternating current (AC) electric current that reverses its direction many times each second. *Compare* DIRECT CURRENT.

amperage the amount of an electric current.

amperes units of measurement of the amount of an electric current.

amplify increase the strength of.

antenna a device that transforms electromagnetic waves into electric current or vice versa.

arc lamp lamp in which electric current jumping, or arcing, from one electrode to another through a gas creates light.

armature the part of an electromechanical machine that carries the current; it may consist of an insulated coil of metal wire, the core around which the wire is wrapped, or both.

battery a device that can store electricity and deliver it as a continuous current.

capacitor a device that accumulates an electric charge and eventually releases it; it consists of two conducting layers separated by an insulating layer. It is also called a CONDENSER.

commutator a device that changes the direction of an electric current; it is attached to the armature in direct-current motors to change incoming alternating current into direct current.

condenser *See* CAPACITOR.

conductor a material that allows the flow of electric current; many metals, for instance, are good conductors. *Compare* INSULATOR.

direct current (DC) electric current that flows in only one direction. *Compare* ALTERNATING CURRENT.

dynamo a device that generates electricity, usually in the form of direct current. *See also* GENERATOR.

electrical oscillator a device that produces electrical current that alternates, or oscillates, at a particular frequency. *Compare* MECHANICAL OSCILLATOR.

electric current   a flow of electrons passing through a conducting material. *See also* CONDUCTOR; ELECTRON.

electromagnetic energy   energy made up of combined electric and magnetic fields. *See also* ELECTROMAGNETIC SPECTRUM.

electromagnetic spectrum   the full range of electromagnetic energy, from gamma rays and X-rays (highest energy, greatest frequency, shortest wavelength) through light to radio waves (lowest energy and frequency, longest wavelength). *See also* ELECTROMAGNETIC ENERGY.

electron   a negatively charged subatomic particle that orbits the nucleus of an atom. *See also* ELECTRIC CURRENT.

fluid   a liquid or gas.

frequency   the number of occurrences of a repeating event (such as the reversal of flow in an alternating electric current, the rising and falling of a wave of electromagnetic energy, or the pulsing of a mechanical vibration) per unit of time.

galvanometer   a device that detects and measures small amounts of electricity.

generator   a device that generates electric current through a combination of motion and a magnetic field. *See also* DYNAMO.

geothermal energy   energy from heat deep within the Earth; it can be used to generate electricity by, for instance, creating steam that turns turbines.

Gramme machine   a device invented by Zénobe-Théophile Gramme in the early 1870s, which could act as either a dynamo or a direct-current electric motor.

harmonics   frequencies of electromagnetic energy that bear certain mathematical relationships to a given frequency; if something resonates with electromagnetic waves of a certain frequency, it will often resonate with that frequency's harmonics as well. *See also* FREQUENCY; RESONANCE.

hydropower   the mechanical power of falling water; it can be used to generate electricity by turning turbines.

induce   to create an electric current in a conductor through the movement of a magnetic field.

induction motor   a alternating-current motor in which power is transferred into an armature by a magnetic field rather than through physical contacts (commutators).

insulator   a material that does not allow the passage of an electric current. *Compare* CONDUCTOR.

ionosphere   the uppermost layer of Earth's atmosphere.

mechanical oscillator   a device powered by electric current that sets up mechanical vibrations of a particular frequency. *Compare* ELECTRICAL OSCILLATOR.

modulate   to modify (change) the frequency or other characteristics of an electromagnetic signal.

particle-beam weapon   a weapon that fires a high-energy beam of atoms or electrons.

polyphase motor   an induction motor that obtains its power from three or more alternating electric currents, all out of phase with one another, which create a continuously rotating magnetic field.

radar   (short for **RA**dio **D**etection **A**nd **R**anging) a technology that sends out low-frequency electromagnetic waves and detects distant objects by capturing and analyzing the waves that are reflected back from the objects.

radio waves   a form of electromagnetic energy with waves longer (of a lower frequency) than those of infrared light (heat).

receiver   a device that receives an electromagnetic signal. *Compare* TRANSMITTER.

resistance   the degree to which a material impedes the passage of an electric current.

resonance   a phenomenon in which one object transfers energy to another without touching it (that is, it sends the energy through some medium, such as air or water) so that the two objects vibrate at the same frequency or at mathematically related frequencies (harmonics). *See also* FREQUENCY; HARMONICS.

robot   a machine either controlled indirectly (by remote control or programming, for example) or capable of acting on its own.

rotor   the part of a motor that moves. *Compare* STATOR.

sonar   a technology, similar to radar, that uses sound waves rather than radio waves to detect distant objects; unlike radar, sonar can operate under water. *See also* RADAR.

spark gap   two electrodes separated by air; when the amount of charge in one electrode becomes great enough, it breaks down the air molecules in the gap and lets the accumulated current leap across the space in the form of a spark.

standing wave   a phenomenon in which each pulse or wave of energy meets and reinforces the wave behind it, creating a wave that appears to stand still yet steadily grows in volume.

static electricity   electricity that builds up on a surface by friction, such as rubbing.

stator   the part of a motor that does not move. *Compare* ROTOR.

teleautomaton   Tesla's name for a device controlled wirelessly by radio or other signals sent from a distance (remote control).

tesla   the unit of magnetic flux density (the strength of a magnetic field).

Tesla coil   a device invented by Nikola Tesla that can act as both a transformer, generating alternating current of exceptionally high voltage, and an electrical oscillator, tuning the current to alternate at particular frequencies. *See also* ELECTRICAL OSCILLATOR; TRANSFORMER.

transformer   a device that raises or lowers the voltage of an alternating electric current by means of a magnetic field. A transformer that raises voltage is called a step-up transformer, and one that lowers voltage is called a step-down transformer.

transmitter   a device that sends out an electromagnetic signal. *Compare* RECEIVER.

turbine   a machine that use the force of a liquid or a gas to turn a central shaft. Most turbines turn the shaft by means of blades, but Tesla invented a turbine that lacks blades.

viscosity   the resistance of a fluid to flow.

voltage   the pressure of an electric current, measured in volts.

volts   units of measurement of the pressure of an electric current.

VTOL (Vertical Takeoff and Landing) aircraft   a fixed-wing or rotor-powered aircraft that can hover and can take off and land vertically.

wattage   the amount of energy in an electric current, measured in watts; it is determined by multiplying the amount of the current (amperage) by the pressure of the current (voltage). *See also* AMPERAGE; VOLTAGE.

watts   units of measurement of the energy in an electric current.

X-ray   a form of electromagnetic wave with high energy, high frequency, and short wavelength.

Further Resources

Books

Cheney, Margaret. *Tesla: Man out of Time*. New York: Simon and Schuster, 1981.

    One of several major biographies of Tesla, somewhat easier to read than those of O'Neill and Seifer.

Jonnes, Jill. *Empires of Light: Edison, Tesla, Westinghouse, and the Race to Electrify the World*. New York: Random House, 2003.

    Well-written account of the war of the currents in the early 1890s, during which the inventors who espoused direct current and those who espoused alternating current struggled for dominance. Includes numerous quotes from contemporary sources.

Martin, Thomas Commerford, ed. *The Inventions, Researches, and Writings of Nikola Tesla*. Charleston, S.C.: Createspace, 2010.

    Reissue of the original collection of Tesla's writings, first published in 1894.

Nye, David E. *Electrifying America: Social Meanings of a New Technology*. Cambridge, Mass.: MIT Press, 1990.

    Describes how the coming of widespread electric power changed American life in the first half of the 20th century.

O'Neill, John J. *Prodigal Genius: The Life of Nikola Tesla*. Kempton, Ill.: Adventures Unlimited Press, 2008.

    Reissue of the first biography of Tesla, written by a Pulitzer Prize–winning science reporter who knew Tesla personally in the inventor's later years.

Seifer, Marc J. *Wizard: The Life and Times of Nikola Tesla*. New York: Kensington Publishing Corp./Citadel Press, 1996.

    Relatively recent biography of Tesla, making use of materials not available to earlier biographers.

Tesla, Nikola. *Colorado Springs Notes, 1899–1900.* Beograd, Yugoslavia: Nolit, 1978.

Text of the notebooks Tesla kept throughout his eventful year at Colorado Springs, during which he proved to his satisfaction that the Earth could transmit signals and electrical power, generated electric currents of immensely high voltages, and heard what he believed was a communication from intelligent beings on another planet.

———. *The Nikola Tesla Treasury.* Radford, Va.: Wilder Publications, 2007.

Contains a large selection of Tesla's scientific and popular writings, including his autobiography.

———. *Very Truly Yours, Nikola Tesla.* Radford, Va.: Wilder Publications, 2009.

A collection of Tesla's letters to the editors of magazines and newspapers on a variety of subjects.

White, Michael. *Acid Tongues and Tranquil Dreamers: Tales of Bitter Rivalry That Fueled the Advancement of Science and Technology.* New York: Harper-Collins/William Morrow, 2001.

Contains a lively chapter on the war of the currents between Tesla/Westinghouse and their rival, Thomas Edison.

Internet Resources

"HAARP: A Premier Facility for the Study of Ionospheric Physics and Radio Science." High Frequency Active Auroral Research Program. Available online. URL: http://www.haarp.alaska.edu. Accessed June 17, 2011.

Web site of a government-sponsored science program that beams high-frequency electromagnetic waves into the ionosphere in order to learn more about natural processes in that layer of the atmosphere and study its interaction with radio signals, subjects that strongly interested Tesla. The site gives an overview of the program and lists some of its findings.

"Inside the Lab." Public Broadcasting System. 2000. Available online. URL: http://www.pbs.org/tesla/ins/index.html. Accessed June 17, 2011.

Describes several of Tesla's most important inventions: the alternating current motor, the Tesla coil, radio, remote control, and improved lighting.

"154 Years from Birth of Nikola Tesla." Tesla Museum. Available online. URL: http://www.tesla-museum.org/meni_en.htm. Accessed June 17, 2011.

Web site of the Tesla Museum in Belgrade, Serbia, includes a brief biography of Tesla and a description of the museum and its collections.

Prince, Cameron B. "Tesla Universe." Tesla Universe. Last updated March 20, 2011. Available online. URL: http://www.teslauniverse.com. Accessed June 17, 2011.

Web site devoted to Tesla-related material. Includes information about the Tesla Coil Builders' Association, a hobbyist group.

Tesla, Nikola. "A Story of Youth Told by Age." Public Broadcasting System. 2000. Available online. URL: http://www.pbs.org/tesla/ll/story_youth.html. Accessed June 17, 2011.

Charming story, originally part of a letter from Tesla to the young daughter of the Yugoslavian ambassador to the United States, that describes Tesla's first encounter with electricity.

"Tesla: Life and Legacy." Public Broadcasting System. 2000. Available online. URL: http://www.pbs.org/tesla/ll/index.html. Accessed June 17, 2011.

Extensive biography of Tesla in 12 sections, intended to accompany a PBS documentary on Tesla originally broadcast on December 12, 2000.

"Tesla: Master of Lightning." Public Broadcasting System. 2000. Available online. URL: http://www.pbs.org/tesla. Accessed June 17, 2011.

Extensive Web site to accompany a documentary originally broadcast on December 12, 2000, includes an extensive biography of Tesla, descriptions of several of his inventions, comments from people whose work is related to Tesla, lesson plans for teachers, lists of articles about Tesla and key Tesla patents, and time lines of discoveries related to electricity and radio.

"Tesla Society Switzerland & EU." Available online. URL: http://www.tesla-society.ch. Accessed June 17, 2011.

Lists recent events honoring or related to Tesla. In German.

"Tesla Wardenclyffe Project." Tesla Wardenclyffe Project. Last updated April 19, 2010. Available online. URL: http://www.teslascience.org. Accessed June 17, 2011.

Web site of a group who are trying to preserve the Tesla laboratory building at the Wardenclyffe site on Long Island and turn it into a museum honoring Tesla.

Vujovic, Ljuba. "Nikola Tesla, the Genius Who Lit the World." Tesla Memorial Society of New York. July 10, 1998. Available online. URL: http://www.teslasociety.com/biography.htm. Accessed June 17, 2011.

Fairly detailed biography of Tesla.

"Welcome to the Tesla Memorial Society of New York Website." Tesla Memorial Society of New York. Available online. URL: http://www.teslasociety.com/index.html. Accessed June 17, 2011.

Web site of the Tesla Memorial Society of New York includes photographs and a biography of Tesla, brief information on his most important inventions, links to articles about or related to Tesla, and links to other Tesla Web sites.

"WiTricity." WiTricity. Last updated 2010. Available online. URL: http://www.witricity.com. Accessed June 17, 2011.

Web site of company established in 2007 by MIT physics professor Marin Soljačić and his coworkers to develop short-distance wireless transmission of electric power. The site explains how the MIT scientists transmit power and how their procedure is like and different from Tesla's.

Zyga, Lisa. "Bladeless Wind Turbine Inspired by Tesla." PhysOrg.com. May 7, 2010. Available online. URL: http://www.physorg.com/news192426996.html. Accessed June 17, 2011.

Article describes a modern wind turbine created by Solar Aero, a New Hampshire-based company, that uses Tesla's bladeless turbine design.

Periodicals

Berardinis, Larry. "Waverunner." *Motion System Design* 47–48 (October 2005–April 2006): 6–8.

Biographical sketch and tribute to Tesla in six short parts.

Flore, Kristina. "Reviving Tesla's Wireless Power Initiatives." *Electronic Design* 55 (September 13, 2007): 21–22.

Brief article about WiTricity, MIT researchers' attempt to produce wireless transfer of electric power over short distances, fulfilling one of Tesla's major dreams.

Hall, Stephen S. "Tesla: A Scientific Saint, Wizard or Carnival Sideman?" *Smithsonian* 71 (June 1986): 120–130.

Meaty biographical article about Tesla, illustrated with numerous photos.

Jacobs, Derek. "Why Tesla?" *Physics Review* 16 (April 2007): 28–29.

Brief review of Tesla's achievements and why he was important.

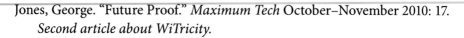
Jones, George. "Future Proof." *Maximum Tech* October–November 2010: 17.

Second article about WiTricity.

Kisslinger, Jerry. "The Fathers of Invention." *A&E Monthly,* October 1995: 44–47.

Describes the rivalry between Tesla and Thomas Edison and compares their qualities as inventors.

Index